W9-ARN-591

CLASSIC CAKES
AND COOKIES

by Barbara Maher
Illustrated by Ken Laidlaw

PANTHEON BOOKS • NEW YORK

First American Edition

Text Copyright © 1986 by Barbara Maher
Illustrations Copyright © 1986 by Walker Books, Ltd.

All rights reserved under International and Pan-American
Copyright Conventions. Published in the United States by
Pantheon Books, a division of Random House, Inc.,
New York, and simultaneously in Canada by
Random House of Canada Limited, Toronto.
Originally published in Great Britain
by Walker Books, Ltd., London, in 1986.

Library of Congress Cataloging-in-Publication Data
Maher, Barbara.
Classic cakes and cookies

(A Pantheon classic cookbook)
Originally published: London:
Walker Books, 1986.
Includes index.
1. Cake. 2. Pastry. I. Title. II. Series.
TX771.M314   1987   641.8'653   86-30506
ISBN 0-394-56167-8

Printed in Italy

CONTENTS

INTRODUCTION

It is to northern and central Europe that we turn for our inspiration in the baking kitchen today, and the influences of Austria and France in particular have now been established throughout most of the world. But much of this tradition has its roots in the Middle East.

The ancient Egyptians baked breads and pastries made of eggs and milk sweetened with honey and flavored, in later times, with exotic spices, nuts, orange-flower and rose waters; their favorite flavors they became highly desirable commodities. A Spice Road across land and sea from China, India, and Ceylon to the eastern Mediterranean opened up, and the Arabs developed a highly lucrative trade. In the eleventh century the crusaders brought the unfamiliar ingredients further north into Europe, and the new, sweetly spiced Middle Eastern delicacies quickly gained in popularity.

The monks now began to play an important role in the development of European baking. Behind the peaceful monastic walls during the difficult and violent Middle Ages, they continued tending their flocks, keeping bees, and nurturing their produce of herbs, vegetables, and fruit trees. They also enjoyed experimenting with the new spices and gained respect for their fine cuisine and bakery. Spiced honey cakes were particularly popular.

The port of Venice, in northern Italy, was emerging as the principal trading point with the Orient for spices and the other unusual ingredients. The Italians assimilated the exotic eastern cooking techniques and Arab-spiced meats, poultry, and fish, stuffed vegetables and pastries wrapped around dried fruits and sweet-almond and pistachio fillings appeared on their tables. Ice creams and sorbets, too, were popular, as were plain doughs soaked in syrup.

With the betrothal of Catherine de Médicis and the future King of France, Henry II, in the mid-sixteenth century, Italy's important initiative in the new cooking began to decline. The Italian chefs of the new queen introduced to their French colleagues the Oriental flavoring and techniques, and the French quickly adopted them as their own. In a short time the style of manners and eating of the French court became the most influential authority, to be emulated by all the major courts and cities of northern Europe. Cooking and baking took on new importance and came to be regarded as one of the civilized arts—a situation that remains little changed today.

But while the accolade for savory cuisine must remain with France, the finest sweet confectionery undoubtedly comes from the Austro-Hungarian Empire, where it reached its zenith early in the nineteenth century, when the indulgence in sweets was at an excess. Earlier, in the seventeenth and eighteenth centuries, luxurious cakes and pastries had graced only the tables of the aristocracy throughout Europe, and the less affluent had baked with the luxury commodities only for festive and celebratory events; but with the fall in sugar prices and as spices and nuts became more readily available, most people were able to afford them. Sweet confectionery now became part of the general diet.

Each European country has its own classics in baking, and although some recipes, such as pound cake, may bear a resemblance to each other, the individual styles are quite pronounced. Britain always tended to prefer plainer fare: wafers, gingerbread and pies, biscuits and simple yeasted bread doughs, sometimes lightly fruited and in later times more heavily so.

In nineteenth-century France at the time of Carême, their most famous chef, cakes were built up into huge and elaborate centerpieces. The foundation of these "pièces montées" was made of simple sponge cakes or marzipan and was lavishly decorated and arranged to represent particular articles or scenes, with scant regard for flavor or texture. Nevertheless the baking style of France has exerted a strong influence, and variations of sponge cake, choux pastry, meringue, and fruit tarts are highly popular throughout the world.

Tastes in confectionery in the central European lands are very similar, but there are regional differences. Germany is especially fond of yeasted cakes and also nut cakes. Rum and kirsch are favorite flavorings; and fruits are used extensively, particularly in the south. Switzerland has similar tastes, though sometimes Swiss cakes incline to a slight heaviness. Austria and Hungary have the most exciting fare. Ranging from small, traditional nut-filled yeast crescents and Arab-style strudels to lavish cream-filled layer cakes that have now been adopted by the rest of the world as after-dinner extravaganzas, their cakes are a sympathetic blend of flavors and textures, appealing to the eye and the palate.

This book offers a wide selection of some of the best-loved and lesser-known classic cakes of the world. It is divided into five chapters. The first is concerned with basic preparations. The second includes simple fare suitable for serving with a cup of coffee or tea— small biscuits, easy tea breads, and plain cakes. Cakes for afternoon tea and high tea are more substantial and richer than those in the earlier section. There are scones and griddle cakes from Scotland and a selection of tarts, traditional yeasted cakes, and richer plain cakes. After-dinner desserts include the layered cakes so popular in Austro-Hungarian cuisine as well as fruit flans and cream sponges. Festival cakes throughout the continents are invariably spiced and filled with dried fruits and nuts; it is interesting to see the variety in this section, despite the similarity of ingredients.

Barbara Maher

SELECTION OF INGREDIENTS
FOR BAKING

Good-quality ingredients are the foundation of good cooking and of good baking too.

Choose fresh, **free-range eggs** if possible; they generally have a bright-yellow yolk and a finer flavor than battery-fed eggs. Crack the egg open and the yolk will be trapped in the middle of a firm, transparent white; if the white is thin and runny, the egg is old and the flavor stale. Use large eggs in the recipes unless otherwise stated.

Use only **butter**; it is a must for baking, because margarine has less flavor.

Most recipes use **all-purpose flour** (preferably unbleached) with the addition of baking powder when a greater leaven is needed. Bread flour (if you can get it) is recommended for yeast doughs because of its greater gluten content. It is more elastic than all-purpose flour and helps the yeast cells grow well, giving a good rise to the cake or bread.

Potato flour is made from potatoes that are boiled and sieved before being dried. The texture is fine and dense, like cornstarch, but its flavor is distinctively creamy and nutty. Sift well before using.

Superfine sugar is ideal for baking since it dissolves more quickly than coarser sugars. Use **granulated sugar** for making syrups. **Confectioners' sugar** must always be sifted, for lumps will not disperse once they are combined with other ingredients.

When using **brown sugars,** follow recipe instructions precisely. Do not substitute white sugar for brown, as brown is moister, and has a stronger flavor, so it could spoil the cake.

Fresh **nuts** are essential in baking. Stale nuts are inclined to rancidity, which taints and spoils a cake completely. Look for dates on packages. Blanch raw **almonds** by dropping them into boiling water for 2–3 minutes; drain and slip off the brown skins. Spread them out on a baking sheet and dry in a 275°F oven for about half an hour. Grind when cold, taking care

not to overgrind, which will release the bitter oils. If using purchased ready-ground almonds, the flavor may be enhanced by adding a drop or two of orange-flower or rose water.

Choose **walnuts** with care; their shelf life is relatively short. Take care grinding them, for they are the most oily of nuts, and the oil is easily released, with distasteful consequences.

Toast **hazelnuts** in a 350°F oven for about 10 minutes. When they start to brown and the skins flake and split, lift the baking sheet from the oven and rub a few nuts at a time in a tea towel or coarse cloth. Discard the skins and allow to cool. Alternatively, buy ready-ground nuts, if appropriate.

Choose only the best-quality **plain or bitter chocolate**, either imported cooking or baker's chocolate or unsweetened dessert chocolate. To melt chocolate, break it up into pieces and drop them into a small bowl set over lightly simmering water. The bowl must not touch the water. Allow to melt without stirring.

Use as directed in the recipes.

The **vanilla pod**, an aromatic shiny, black pod with numerous seeds, is used extensively in European baking. Use the pod whole as an infusion in liquids; wash it in cold water after use, dry carefully and use again. The pod is split and the seeds are scraped out for flavoring cakes.

To make **vanilla sugar**, reserve scraped vanilla pods and plunge them into a tightly stoppered jar of superfine sugar. Two or three 1½-inch pieces are enough to perfume 2 pounds sugar. Top the jar up with more sugar as it is used.

Orange-flower water and rose water are subtle perfumes with a Middle-Eastern flavor. Use them with discretion.

Apricot jam is used to give flavor and to insulate cake crumbs from icing decorations. To make a glaze, gently heat about ½ cup apricot jam with 2 tablespoons water until slightly thickened. Strain through a sieve and brush the jam over the cake while still warm.

PREPARATION FOR BAKING

All ingredients should be at room temperature before starting preparation. Because of the accuracy required in baking, everything should be measured out precisely. Please keep to the quantities given in each recipe.

Butter the cake pan and line it if necessary.

To line a cake for a sponge cake, use wax or parchment paper. Cut a circle to fit snugly in to the base of the pan. Lightly butter the paper and sides of the pan, then dust with a mixture of equal parts of superfine sugar and flour over all.

For a heavy, fruited cake batter the sides of the pan also need to be lined. Use two layers of brown paper first, then one of wax parchment paper, as above. Cut brown wax paper and strips for the sides of the pan about 2 inches higher than the edge to stand as a protective collar. If you grease the pan first, it will help hold the paper in place, then grease the paper base and sides well with melted butter.

Preheat the oven and check that the temperature is correct, using an oven thermometer if in doubt. In most instances a cake is put into the oven as soon as the batter is ready. Do not open the oven door until at least three-quarters of the recommended baking time has elapsed.

Test a cake for doneness by inserting a clean skewer or wooden toothpick into the center; it should come out clean and dry. If any mixture still adheres, let the cake bake a little longer. The cake should have risen well, browned, and be shrinking away slightly from the sides of the pan.

Cook the cake on a wire rack, either in the pan or turned out, depending on the recipe instruction. Air must be allowed to circulate around the base of the pan so that the cake does not become soggy or collapse.

KEEPING CAKES

Cakes should be wrapped closely in foil or stored in an airtight tin. Cream-filled ones must be kept in the refrigerator.

Butter-cream-filled cakes and sponges may be frozen quite successfully. Place the cake on an open tray in the freezer. As soon as it has frozen through, wrap tightly in foil or plastic wrap and replace in the freezer. Store a cake for no more than about 1–2 months, or the flavor will be spoiled. Defrost at room temperature for up to 3 hours or in the refrigerator overnight.

For freezing yeasted cakes, see p. 17.

UTENSILS

Electric mixers may be used for making many cakes in this book; the batter will be beaten more thoroughly

and be better aerated. If the recipe calls for egg whites to be whipped separately, an electric mixer may be used, but the whites should still be folded in by hand, otherwise the beaten-in air will be lost.

A dough hook on a mixer is also very useful for beating a basic yeast mixture. When the mixture starts to throw large pockets of air, turn it out onto a lightly floured work surface and knead for a few moments longer. Fruits and nuts should be kneaded in by hand, since such dough is too heavy for a home mixer to handle.

Food processors are more limited in their use. They make excellent pastry and yeasted doughs; nuts may be ground well; and butter creams are easy to whip. But cakes are less successful, for it is more difficult to aerate a batter satisfactorily. Avoid beating egg whites with this.

Apart from the more common baking utensils, there are a few used in this book that are less familiar in the ordinary kitchen.

Gugelhupf mold: a sculptured, traditional shape with a funneled center and slanting sides.

Madeleine sheet: usually 12 small scallop-shell-shaped bun molds.

Balmoral: a guttered cake pan, usually 12 inches in length (sometimes known as Rehrücken), half round and ribbed.

Springform pan: conventional round shape with a loose base and a clip on the side which releases to unmold the cake. This is a most versatile, multipurpose pan and may be bought in various sizes and also with a plain savarin funnel or a border pattern.

Copper bowl: a luxury item, but it gives the best results for beating egg whites.

Copper sugar boiler: a straight-sided pan with a lip for pouring made of untinned copper. Copper is the best material for conducting heat rapidly.

KNOW YOUR OVEN

A correct oven temperature is essential for baking success. The temperatures indicated for each recipe in this book are approximate, since every oven varies; they are for a regular oven where the heat source lies at one or other point in the oven. Fan-assisted and convection ovens work on a different principle; the heat that is circulated by a fan is more even, which seems to make the temperature hotter. There is so little variance in the heat throughout the oven that cakes incline to cook more quickly and to dry out. It may be necessary to reduce the oven temperature by plus or minus 50°, but please consult your oven literature for precise instruction.

An oven thermometer is helpful to establish whether an oven is heating correctly or not.

1
BASIC RECIPES

SWEET SHORTCRUST PASTRY

FOR A 9½-INCH FLAN OR 14 TARTLETS

1¼ cups flour	2 tablespoons superfine
pinch of salt	sugar
¼ pound butter, chilled	1 egg, lightly beaten
and cubed	2 tablespoons ice water

Sift the flour and salt into a large bowl; drop in the pieces of butter and, using the fingertips, lightly rub the fat with the flour to make a crumb texture. Fork in the sugar, egg, and 1 tablespoon of the water. Lightly combine all the ingredients into a smooth pastry. Add a little more water if necessary; the texture should be soft but not sticky. Roll into a ball.

Working with a small piece of pastry at a time and using the heel of the hand, blend the pastry thoroughly by pushing it away from you on the lightly floured work surface; it should be smooth and pliable. Gather the pieces of pastry into a ball, lightly dust with flour, wrap tightly, and chill for at least 30 minutes before using.

This pastry is very elastic and must be left to rest for a few minutes after being rolled out and before lining the pan.

Baking blind: The pastry case is baked to a crisp shell without a filling. It may then be lined with pastry cream (p. 70) and heaped with fresh, soft fruits.

Prepare the pastry as above, rolling it out about ¼ inch thick and a little larger than the flan tin. Allow to rest for a few minutes to let it shrink back.

Using a rolling pin, lift the pastry over the buttered tin and gently ease it into place. Patch any tears if need be—the appearance will not be spoiled. Smooth away any air bubbles and trim the edges neatly. Make sure that the pastry on the top rim of the tin is quite thick, so that it does not brown too quickly. Prick the pastry base all over with a fork. Cover the surface with a sheet of wax paper and weigh it down with ceramic pebbles or dried beans. Bake on a preheated baking sheet to give a good crispy base to the flan at 400°F for 10 minutes, then reduce the heat to 350°F for about 20 minutes. Five minutes before the baking is complete, remove the paper and weights from the flan case and carefully brush the whole of the pastry surface with lightly beaten egg white. Return the flan to the oven for 5 minutes more to dry out and seal the surface.

Parbaking a flan case: Occasionally it is necessary to parbake a pastry flan for a short while before it is filled.

When the tin has been lined with pastry, cover the base and sides with a sheet of wax paper and weigh down with pebbles or dried beans. Bake in a preheated 400°F oven for 10–15 minutes, or until the pastry has set and colored slightly. Carefully remove the paper and weights and fill as instructed.

FAT-FREE SPONGE

There are two methods of preparing fat-free sponges. The classic method prepared over heat is golden colored with quite a dense texture, while the cold method produces a paler, more aerated sponge. Both sponges will keep fresh for 2–3 days but freeze well for up to 2 months. Defrost at room temperature for 2–3 hours.

FOR A 9½-INCH CAKE PAN

4 eggs	2 inches vanilla pod, split
½ cup superfine sugar	scant ¾ cup flour, sifted

350°F: 30–35 minutes for 1 large sponge;
20 minutes for 2 shallow cakes.

THE CLASSIC METHOD

A sponge batter without fat is traditionally beaten over heat. The best results are achieved using a balloon whisk, but almost as good a result may be obtained using a hand-held electric beater.

Line the bottom of a 9½-inch springform pan or 2 9½-inch cake pans with parchment paper, butter, and dredge with a mixture of equal amounts of superfine sugar and flour. Break the eggs into a large heatproof bowl and beat in the sugar. Set the bowl over a pan of simmering water, taking care that the base does not actually come in contact with it, and beat the mixture as it warms until it changes to a pale and creamy froth. It will have expanded to almost twice its bulk.

Lift the bowl off the heat and continue beating while it cools down. The volume will increase to about three times, and a thick ribbon of batter will fall off the whisk and hold a trail in the mixture for at least 5 seconds.

Scrape the vanilla seeds from the pod and mix them in. Sift one-third of the flour and fold it in lightly, using a metal spoon. Cut down and back up through the mixture in a figure-eight movement, rotating the bowl as you work and making sure that all parts of the mixture are incorporated. Avoid stirring, which results in a soggy, heavy cake. Continue with the two other thirds of flour in the same way.

Pour the sponge mixture straight into the prepared baking pan. Tap the pan sharply on the work surface once to disperse any air pockets, and bake immediately.

When the cake is well risen and golden colored, test with a skewer; it should come out clean. The cake will also be shrinking away very slightly from the edges of the pan. Lift the cake out of the oven and allow it to settle in the pan for 5 minutes on a wire rack. Invert the cake onto the rack and allow to cool.

THE COLD METHOD

In this method a cold batter is prepared with the egg yolks and sugar, and the separately beaten egg whites are folded in last of all.

Carefully separate the eggs. Reserve 2 tablespoons sugar and beat the remainder with the egg yolks into a pale creamy mass. The mixture should fall from the whisk in a thick ribbon and will at least have doubled in bulk. Scrape the vanilla seeds from the pod and mix in.

Whisk the egg whites in a separate bowl until they stand in soft, snowy peaks; dredge over the reserved sugar and continue beating until the meringue has a thin, glossy texture. Mix 2 tablespoons of meringue with the yolk batter to lighten it, then, alternating with siftings of flour, carefully fold in the rest of the meringue. Finish in the same way as for the classic method.

GENOESE SPONGE

Genoese sponge keeps fresh for up to 1 week, and while it is basically the same as a fat-free sponge, butter is added, which improves the keeping qualities. The butter is folded in at the final stage.

FOR A 9½-INCH CAKE PAN

4 eggs	2 inches vanilla pod, split
scant ⅔ cup superfine sugar	¼ pound unsalted butter, melted and cooled
¾ cup flour, sifted	

350°F: 45 minutes.

Prepare the basic sponge either over heat or by the cold method, as described in the previous recipe. Finish off by folding in the melted butter, in three stages, taking care to exclude any sediment in the bottom of the pan. Turn the batter into the prepared pan and bake.

YEAST DOUGHS

Types of yeast

Yeast doughs are most successful made with **fresh yeast**. The yeast should look moist, creamy, and beige-white-colored and should cut in a block. Once it starts to crumble and darken, the freshness has been lost.

Dried yeast is a good alternative. Look for the date mark on the package, since the shelf life lasts no more than a year. Dried yeast is concentrated, and half the quantity stipulated for fresh yeast should be used.

Fresh and dried yeast must be dissolved before being added to a cake mixture; see Yeast Sponge Batter below. The yeast should be combined with a small amount of sugar, flour, and liquid taken from the main recipe.

Quick-rising yeast granules are not dissolved in a liquid, but blended directly into the main ingredients. They are most successful for making plain breads but less reliable with enriched doughs that include large quantities of eggs, butter, sugar, and dried fruits. Follow the instructions on the package if you want to substitute them.

Yeast sponge batter

Continental yeast cakes generally contain a greater quantity of enriching ingredients than most British bread doughs. To encourage a lively reaction from the yeast, it is essential to prepare a preliminary sponge batter with part of the ingredients taken from the main

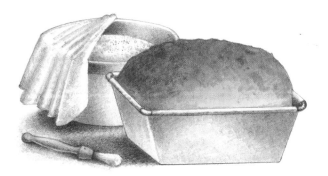

recipe. All the ingredients should be at room temperature before preparation starts. The flour may also be warmed slightly in a low oven, since that encourages the yeast cells to grow.

Warm the liquid to tepid (80°F). Crumble the fresh or dried yeast into the liquid in a warm bowl, add 1 teaspoon of sugar taken from the main recipe. Stir until the yeast has dissolved. Mix in about a quarter of the flour and beat vigorously to disperse any lumps and encourage fermentation. Cover with a warm, floured cloth and let rise for 10–15 minutes. The batter should swell and foam to about twice its volume before being used.

If the reaction of the yeast batter is lethargic, throw it away, since the yeast must be stale.

Kneading the dough

Yeast dough needs considerable beating and kneading, once all the basic ingredients have been blended, to encourage a lively yeast activity and give lightness and a fine texture.

At first the dough is rather sticky and difficult to handle, but the more it is worked, the easier it becomes, and eventually it will start to roll off the sides of the bowl into a smooth, silky mass that is very elastic and throws large pockets of air. Cover the bowl with a floured cloth and let rise and prove in a warm place. When the dough has doubled in volume, knock it back by punching and kneading for a few moments. Add the remaining enriching ingredients, form into a finished shape or place in the prepared mold, cover, and let rise again for a short while. Bake in a preheated oven.

Handling yeast—main points to watch

Use fresh yeast if possible.

Use strong white flour; this improves the rise because of its higher gluten content and greater elasticity.

Warm all the ingredients before preparation.

Do not heat the liquid to more than 80°F, or the yeast cells may be killed.

Yeast pastries are generally prepared in three stages. A preliminary yeast sponge, followed by two proving

or rising periods. These improve the quality of the dough.

The covered yeast dough should rise in a draft-free spot with a steady temperature of no more than 80°F.

Use unsalted butter to grease warmed pans, then dust with flour.

Never open the oven door until at least 30 minutes of the baking time has elapsed; a draft will cause the cake to collapse.

A yeast cake tastes best the day it is made. It may be frozen while still slightly warm. Slip it into a plastic bag and seal to prevent drying out and going stale.

Yeast dough keeps up to 2 months in the freezer. Defrost at room temperature for 2–3 hours.

COOKED BUTTER CREAM WITH SUGAR SYRUP

A firm butter cream made with egg yolks that will hold its shape in warm weather.

FOR A 9½-INCH CAKE

½ cup granulated sugar	1 cup unsalted butter,
4 egg yolks, lightly beaten	softened and beaten until
1 drop of vanilla extract	smooth

Pour 5 tablespoons water into a heavy-based pan or copper sugar boiler, add the sugar, and warm gently until all the sugar has dissolved. Bring to a brisk boil and cook to the thread stage (225°F). This takes about 20 seconds after boiling starts. Dip scissor points into the syrup, lift them out, and open them: thin threads should form.

Dip the base of the pan briefly in cold water to stop the cooking, then pour the syrup in a slow, steady stream onto the egg yolks, beating all the time. Add the vanilla and continue whisking until the cream has cooled completely and is light and foamy. Beat a spoonful at a time of egg-yolk cream into the butter. Cover and let set in the refrigerator, where it keeps fresh for up to a week.

FLAVORS FOR BUTTER CREAM

Brandy, rum, or kirsch: add 2 tablespoons of chosen flavor to the cooked cream before blending with the butter.

Coffee and chocolate: melt and cool 3½ ounces plain dark chocolate. Dissolve 1 tablespoon instant coffee powder or granules in ½ tablespoon boiling water. Stir together, let cool, then blend into the finished cream.

Citrus: blend 2 tablespoons of strained fresh orange or lemon juice into the cooked cream before blending with the butter.

BUTTER CREAM

FOR A 9½-INCH CAKE

¾ cup confectioners' sugar, sifted	7 ounces (1 stick plus 6 tablespoons) unsalted butter, softened
3 egg yolks	

Sift the sugar into a bowl, add the egg yolks, and beat in the butter. Mix in a flavoring (see previous recipe) and beat well until thoroughly blended and smooth. Chill until needed. It will keep fresh for up to a week in the refrigerator and in the freezer for several weeks. Defrost at room temperature for 3–4 hours.

GLACÉ ICING

Glacé icing is easily prepared, but sets very quickly. Before making the icing, prepare the cake. Set it on a wire rack with a sheet of wax paper underneath to catch any drips. Trim the cake level if need be, and coat carefully with warmed and strained apricot jam (p. 11) to insulate the crumb surface. On one side, lay out any decorations in the correct pattern so that they may be placed straight onto the wet icing before it sets.

FOR A 9½-INCH CAKE

2¼ cups confectioners' sugar, sifted	5 drops of vanilla extract
4–5 tablespoons almost-boiling water	

Sift the sugar into a small heatproof bowl and make a well in the middle using a wooden spoon. Slowly add the water and flavoring, gently stirring all the time. Avoid adding too much liquid at once, for the icing may become too runny. It should be thick and smooth enough to coat the back of a spoon.

Place the bowl over a small pan one-quarter filled with simmering water, and warm the icing until it thins out and runs easily from the spoon. Remove from the heat and use immediately.

Pour almost all the icing onto the center of the cake. (Replace the bowl over the simmering water to prevent the rest setting.)

Working quickly with a long, dry spatula or kitchen knife, smooth the icing from the middle to the edges of the cake. Avoid spilling over the sides and do not try to rework the surface, for it sets too rapidly and the appearance will be spoiled. Coat the sides of the cake with the reserved icing. Decorate immediately.

FLAVORS FOR GLACÉ ICING
Liquid flavors should be substituted for the water.

Punch: 1 tablespoon fresh orange juice, strained; 1 tablespoon fresh lemon juice, strained; 2½ tablespoons dark rum.

Orange or lemon: 4–5 tablespoons orange or lemon juice, strained.

Coffee: 3 teaspoons instant coffee powder or granules dissolved in 4–5 tablespoons boiling water.

Chocolate: 2 teaspoons cocoa powder and 1 teaspoon instant coffee powder dissolved in 4–5 tablespoons boiling water.

CHOCOLATE ICING

This icing is easier to handle than most and sets with a high gloss that dulls slightly after 24 hours. An iced cake will keep very well for several days in the refrigerator; the chocolate covering will not spoil.

FOR A 9½-INCH CAKE

½ tablespoon unsalted butter	½ cup granulated sugar
3½ ounces plain dark chocolate, broken into pieces	

Set a heatproof bowl over a pan of simmering water and drop in the butter, chocolate pieces, and a tablespoon of water. Melt gently and stir to blend. Lift the bowl off the heat. Measure ¾ cup water into a heavy-based pan and add the sugar, taking care not to let any grains stick to the sides of the pan. Dissolve the sugar slowly, over low heat, then increase the temperature and boil to the thread stage, 225°F (p. 18).

Draw the pan aside and quickly stir in the melted chocolate. Replace the pan over the heat and gently boil the syrup for 5 minutes. The icing will thicken. Test a few drops on a clean plate; it should feel a little sticky.

Leave to cool for a few moments before using, then pour it straight over the apricot-glazed cake surface (p. 11), starting in the middle and working outward in a circular motion. Tip the wire rack on which the cake rests back and forth so that the surface is covered. Avoid using a spatula on the cake top, but smooth some of the chocolate icing on the sides. Apply nuts or any other decorations immediately, but piped icing should be left until the glaze has cooled completely and set. Use a contrasting color for the best effect. Coffee- and chocolate-flavored butter cream (p. 18) may also be used.

— 2 —
THE MORNING BREAK

In Europe, and in Vienna in particular, it was fashionable to drink coffee in a coffeehouse. The tradition began as early as the seventeenth century, not long after the Turks besieged the city and were well and truly trounced—and were also deprived of the coffee they had brought with them. Coffeehouses became the regular meeting places, mainly for men, to discuss the news and read the papers, gossip a little, play chess and billiards, and of course drink coffee, often served with a topping of whipped cream. A small selection of cakes and pastries was offered as well.

A little later chocolate and coffee became the smart new beverages in Britain, too, and were often served with enriched breads spread with butter, for an early repast. Coffeehouses soon became popular in Britain and, as in Vienna, were the regular meeting places for men to discuss their business affairs. Indeed, many clubs and famous institutions were founded there. It was not the custom in Britain to offer cakes and biscuits, although chocolate was drunk, and later tea was served.

Today both tea and coffee have become ubiquitous, although more tea is drunk in Britain than in either Europe or America, where coffee is the preferred beverage. A light snack—a biscuit or a slice of simple cake—is a natural accompaniment. A "coffee morning" has also become a social occasion for friends to get together, but more often it is associated with a charitable function.

All the recipes in this section have the advantage of keeping well. They may be baked several days in advance and stay fresh stored in an airtight container for at least 2 weeks. They are not suitable for freezing. Bake several at a time and you will always have a tempting tidbit to offer.

OLD-FASHIONED POUND CAKE

Pound cake may be found in many European countries and is probably one of the earliest unfruited plain cakes to have been recorded. The name derives from the equal weights of the ingredients. In the past it was necessary to beat the cake for an "hour with your hand or a great wooden spoon" but now an electric mixer makes the task much easier, and the cake is lighter in texture, particularly if part of the beaten egg whites are folded into the batter at the end.

While an English pound cake is traditionally baked in a straight-sided pan, Austrian and German versions are often baked in a gugelhupf shape (p. 13). This mold is sculptured with sloping sides and has a central funnel that allows the heat to penetrate better to the middle of the cake.

MAKES ABOUT 16 SLICES

1⅔ cups flour	4 large eggs
1 teaspoon baking powder	1 teaspoon lemon zest
1 cup butter, softened	2 tablespoons slivered almonds
1⅓ cups superfine sugar	2 tablespoons raisins

350°F: 1¼ hours.

Sift the flour and baking powder together twice, to aerate well. Set aside. Beat the butter and 1 cup of the sugar until pale and fluffy, then whisk in 2 whole eggs until the mixture is well blended. Separate the 2 remaining eggs and beat in the yolks. Add the lemon zest.

Again sift one-third of the flour mixture and beat it in, but only until it has just blended. Overbeating will produce a heavy and stodgy cake. Beat in the remaining flour in two additional portions.

Beat the 2 egg whites until stiff, sift over the rest of the sugar, and whisk for a few moments longer until the mixture is glossy. Lighten the main cake batter by beating in 2 tablespoons of the beaten whites, then gently fold in the remainder of the whites using a large metal spoon.

Butter an 8–8½-inch mold and embed the almonds and raisins around the sides. Pour in the cake batter, smooth the top, and bake in the preheated oven. Let settle in the pan for 10 minutes before turning it out to cool on a wire rack.

VARIATIONS
The uncooked pound cake batter may be enriched in a number of ways.

Chocolate and Coffee Marble Cake
Omit the almonds and raisins when preparing the mold.

Pour half the basic batter into the cake mold as above; blend 2 tablespoons sifted cocoa powder and 1 tablespoon instant coffee powder into the remainder of the mixture and combine well. Pour this over the batter in the pan, level the surface, then gently drag a fork through the center in a swirling motion, to create a marbled effect.

Pound Cake with Fresh Fruit
The basic pound cake tastes particularly good covered with a layer of fresh-cut fruits. It will keep fresh for 2–3 days. You may use a conventional round plain or 9½-inch springform pan.

Use 1 recipe pound cake batter to 1½ pounds small cooking plums, cooking apples, or fresh apricots.

Wash and dry the fruit carefully. Halve and pit the plums or apricots; peel, core, and thickly slice the apples. Pour the prepared cake batter into the buttered mold and pack in the chosen fruit tightly on the surface; pitted fruits should be laid with skins uppermost. The fruits sink to the middle of the cake during baking. Bake in the preheated oven, as above. Test with a skewer when risen and golden. It may take a little longer because of the moisture in the fruits. Leave in the pan to settle for about 15 minutes before turning out to cool.

SUGAR COOKIES

These simple cookies are fun for the whole family to make. Cut them up into different shapes and enjoy their crisp and crunchy sugared texture.

MAKES 40 COOKIES

1½ cups flour, sifted	1 small egg, lightly beaten
7 ounces butter, cubed	**To finish**
½ cup superfine sugar	1 egg, lightly beaten
½ teaspoon lemon zest	granulated sugar

375°F: 20 minutes.

Lightly rub the flour and butter to a fine crumb texture. Stir in the sugar and the lemon zest. Gradually draw a little of the egg at a time into the mixture and knead into a smooth pastry. Add a little more egg if it is too dry. Wrap and chill for 30 minutes.

Roll the pastry out to ⅛ inch thickness and cut out shapes with pastry cutters. Lay the cookies on buttered and floured baking sheets, brush each with beaten egg, and sprinkle a little granulated sugar over.

Bake until golden, and let cool on a wire rack. These cookies keep fresh for at least 2 weeks stored in an airtight container.

SHORTBREAD COOKIES

MAKES 30 COOKIES

1⅔ cups flour	1 egg yolk
pinch of salt	½ teaspoon lemon juice
6 ounces butter, cubed	superfine sugar
¾ cup confectioners' sugar, sifted	

400°F: 10 minutes.

Sift the flour and salt together twice and finally into a large bowl. Drop in the butter pieces and lightly rub to make a crumb texture. Blend in the confectioners' sugar, then add the egg yolk and lemon juice and knead into a smooth dough.

Roll into a long sausage shape about 1½ inches in diameter, dredge with superfine sugar, wrap, and chill for 1 hour. Slice into pieces about ½ inch thick and lay on a lightly buttered and floured baking sheet. Bake until lightly colored and transfer to a wire rack to cool.

23

VIENNESE KIPFEL

In Vienna, it has always been the tradition to serve these small yeasted kipfel with coffee. This recipe must be made with fresh yeast, so the preparation differs from that of the other yeast doughs in this book.

MAKES 20 PIECES

2 ounces fresh yeast	**Filling**
2 tablespoons cold milk	5 tablespoons milk
1 cup plus 2 tablespoons bread flour	½ cup walnuts, finely ground
pinch of salt	2 teaspoons lemon zest
7 tablespoons butter, chilled and cut into small cubes	2 tablespoons superfine sugar
2 teaspoons lemon zest	2 ounces unsalted butter, melted and cooled
2 egg yolks	½ tablespoon dark rum
3 tablespoons superfine sugar	**To finish**
	1 egg, lightly beaten

375°F: 20–30 minutes.

First prepare the nut filling. Bring the milk to a boil, remove it from the heat, and stir in the ground walnuts. Leave to infuse for about 15 minutes for the nuts to swell. Add the lemon zest, sugar, and melted butter; blend well and mix in the rum. Set aside to cool.

To make the yeast dough: crumble the yeast into the cold milk and blend well so that it dissolves thoroughly. Sift the flour and salt onto the work surface and drop in the butter pieces. Rub to a coarse crumb mixture. Add the lemon zest, egg yolks, and sugar. Blend lightly, then stir in the yeast mixture. Quickly combine all the ingredients and knead into a fine dough.

Roll the dough out twice, then form into a ball and cut in two. Cover one piece while working with the other. Flour the work surface and the rolling pin and roll the dough to ⅛ inch thickness. Cut into 4-inch squares. Spread a teaspoon of walnut filling across the middle of each square. Using a knife to help you, roll the squares up diagonally from corner to corner into a cylindrical shape, then bend them into crescent shapes and pinch the ends to seal in the filling.

Place the kipfel well apart on a lightly buttered baking sheet and brush with the beaten egg. Cover and let rise in a warm place until doubled in bulk; this takes about 45 minutes to an hour.

Finish the reserved dough in the same way. Bake immediately in the heated oven until well risen and golden. The kipfel taste best if they are eaten the day they are made.

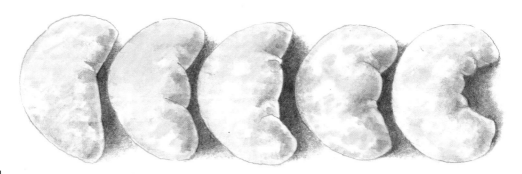

WALNUT SLICES

This recipe originates from an old Scottish friend. It keeps well for about 2 weeks and the fruit and nut topping is a pleasing foil to the short pastry base.

MAKES 18 SLICES

1⅔ cups flour	½ cup (4 ounces) glacé cherries
1 teaspoon baking powder	
¼ pound butter, chilled and cubed	2 tablespoons apricot jam, warmed and strained
¼ cup superfine sugar	¾ cup confectioners' sugar, sifted
1 egg, separated	
1 cup walnuts	granulated sugar

350°F: 45–55 minutes.

Sift the flour and baking powder together twice and finally into a large bowl. Drop in the butter pieces and rub to a fine crumb texture. Stir in the superfine sugar, add the egg yolk, and blend to a smooth dough. Avoid overworking.

Roll into a long rope shape about 1 inch in diameter, cut in half, and lay both pieces on a flat, buttered baking sheet well apart. Press a shallow channel down the center of each strip of pastry with your finger. Prick here and there along the centers with a fork. Set the sheet in the preheated oven and parbake for 15 minutes.

Meanwhile prepare the fruits and nuts. Break the nuts into small pieces; wash the cherries and quarter them. Lift the parbaked pastries from the oven and brush each center channel quite generously with the warm jam. Scatter the fruits and nuts evenly along the surface.

Beat the egg white into snowy peaks, then sift over the confectioners' sugar and continue beating until the meringue is firm and glossy. Spoon the mixture over the fruit and nut channel and slightly roughen the surface with a fork. Dredge with a little granulated sugar to give sparkle.

Bake the pastries for 30–40 minutes more, or until lightly colored. Lift the sheet out of the oven and cut the pastries into slices about 2 inches in length. Transfer immediately to a wire rack to cool. Store in an airtight container.

AUSTRIAN TEA RINGS

These individual sponge rings are very light. They are sandwiched together with apricot jam.

MAKES 24 PIECES

4 egg whites	3 tablespoons butter, melted to lukewarm
scant ½ cup superfine sugar, sifted	
	6 tablespoons apricot jam, warmed and sieved
2 egg yolks, lightly beaten	
1⅔ cups flour	

300°F: 20 minutes.

Beat the egg whites in a large, clean bowl until they hold firm, snowy peaks and the bowl may be inverted without the mixture sliding out. Sift in half the sugar and beat until glossy. Using a large metal spoon, fold in the beaten egg yolks, the rest of the sugar, and a sifting of ¼ cup of the flour; combine carefully. Fold in half the butter and half the remaining flour, followed by the rest of the butter and flour. Avoid stirring the mixture so as not to lose any air.

Fit a large pastry bag with a ¼-inch plain nozzle and pipe small rings, about 1¼ inches in diameter, spaced well apart on buttered and floured baking sheets. Bake immediately. When they are pale gold and well risen, lift out of the oven, transfer to a wire rack, and allow to cool. Sandwich the tea rings in pairs with the apricot jam. Dredge lightly with confectioners' sugar before serving. The cakes stay fresh for no more than 2–3 days.

SWEDISH TEA RING

A coffee- and tea-time favorite in both Britain and America.

MAKES 20 SLICES

2 ounces fresh yeast or ¼ cup dried yeast	⅓ cup currants or sultanas
¼ cup milk, scalded	¾ teaspoon mixed spice
1½ cups bread flour, slightly warmed	4 tablespoons butter, softened
½ teaspoon salt	**Glacé icing**
2 tablespoons superfine sugar	¾ cup confectioners' sugar
1 egg	1–2 tablespoons almost-boiling water
1 egg yolk	1 drop of vanilla extract

400°F: 25–30 minutes.

Crumble the yeast into the heated milk and stir well to dissolve. Cover and set aside to rise and double in bulk. Sift the flour and salt together twice, then into a large mixing bowl. Make a well in the center and drop in 2 tablespoons of the sugar and the egg and egg yolk, which have been lightly beaten together. Draw a little flour from the sides into the middle and blend lightly. Add the yeast liquid. Mix together into a soft, elastic dough, then turn it out onto the floured work surface and continue to work the dough by kneading thoroughly. When it becomes shiny, very elastic, and starts to throw large pockets of air, replace it in the mixing bowl and cover with a tea towel, or place in a lightly oiled large plastic bag. Set to rise in a warm, draft-free place until doubled in bulk, which takes about 1 hour.

Meanwhile stir together the remaining sugar, the currants or sultanas, and the spice. Set aside.

When the dough has risen well, knock it back by kneading for a few moments, then drop it on a lightly floured work surface and roll out into a ¼-inch-thick rectangle. Spread the softened butter in small pats over about two-thirds of it. Fold one-third of the dough over from the short side into the middle and cover it by folding the rest of the dough on top. Firmly press the edges together to seal in the butter pieces, then give the dough a quarter turn to the right. Roll out into a 12-inch square. Distribute the dried-fruit mixture evenly over the surface to about ½ inch from the edges. Dampen the edges of the dough and roll it tightly into a cylinder, pressing the sides together firmly.

Lift the dough onto a large, buttered baking sheet and curl it around into a ring. Use a little water to help join the two ends securely together. With scissors, snip two-thirds of the way through the ring at ½-inch intervals, then press the strips alternately in toward the center and outward. Cover with a lightly floured cloth and allow to rise until doubled in bulk again, about 20–30 minutes. Bake until golden and well risen. Turn out of the pan to cool on a wire rack. Prepare the icing as described on p. 18 and pour it straight over the warm tea ring.

ALMOND-OAT SLICES

MAKES 28 SLICES

7 tablespoons butter	2 cups rolled oats
½ cup soft brown sugar	scant teaspoon ground ginger
½ cup golden syrup or honey	¾ cup slivered almonds

350°F: 20 minutes.

Gently melt the butter in a small pan, together with the sugar and syrup. Remove the pan from the heat, add the oats and ginger, and stir to combine well. Smooth the mixture into a buttered 13½-by-9½-inch jelly roll pan and scatter the slivered almonds over the surface.

Keep a watchful eye while these are baking, for they scorch easily. Lift them out of the oven when they are golden but still feel soft to the touch.

Cut into fingers while still hot and allow to cool in the baking pan. Store in an airtight container.

TUILES

These traditional French almond cookies are wrapped over a rolling pin while still warm so that they have the same curved shape as old roofing tiles. Bake only 4 or 5 at a time and space them well apart on the baking sheet. Work quickly once they have been lifted from the oven.

MAKES 18 COOKIES

⅔ cup ground almonds	2 tablespoons butter, melted and cooled
generous ½ cup superfine sugar	¾ cup slivered almonds, (optional)
1 tablespoon flour	
1 egg white	

325°F: 7–8 minutes.

Stir the almonds, sugar, and flour together in a bowl. Whisk the egg white lightly with a fork and add it to the mixture with the butter. Leave to stiffen in the refrigerator for several hours.

Drop heaped teaspoons of the mixture onto a buttered baking sheet. Flatten each one with the back of a fork to about ⅛-inch thickness. Decorate with a few slivered almonds, if used, and bake until golden.

Lift the cookies from the sheet and lightly press each one over a rolling pin. Leave on the rolling pin to harden for a few minutes before transferring to a wire rack to cool. Store in an airtight container.

MADELEINES

Madeleines were made famous by Marcel Proust, the French author, in his *Remembrance of Things Past*. When he was a child, he visited his aunt on Sunday mornings to take lime tea and madeleines with her. They are always baked in special scallop molds, which may be bought in specialty kitchen shops. You may use plain muffin tins; although madeleines baked in this way may look like ordinary sponge cakes, their flavor is quite subtle and delicate.

MAKES 12 MADELEINES

4 tablespoons unsalted butter	small pinch of salt
2 teaspoons clear honey	½ inch vanilla pod, split and scraped
1 egg	scant ½ cup flour, sifted
3 tablespoons superfine sugar	

350°F: 20 minutes.

Lightly butter and flour the madeleine molds (p. 13). Melt the butter and honey over low heat and allow to cool. Beat together the egg, sugar, and salt until pale and creamy; blend in the scraped vanilla seeds.

Sift one-third of the flour across the surface and, using a large metal spoon, carefully and lightly fold it into the egg mixture, taking care not to lose any air. Fold in about one-third of the butter and honey mixture.

Continue to fold in the flour and butter and honey two more times. Take care not to mix in any of the gritty sediment that lies at the bottom of the butter and honey pan.

Half-fill each of the madeleine molds. Bake until well risen and golden, then turn out onto a wire rack and allow to cool. Madeleines keep well for a few days stored in an airtight container.

LANGUES DE CHAT

CATS' TONGUES

These well-known little French cookies are good served with ice cream, mousses, and other creamy desserts.

MAKES 40

¾ cup flour, sifted	2 egg whites
scant 1 cup confectioners' sugar, sifted	¼ cup superfine sugar
½ cup heavy cream	

400°F: 10 minutes.

Sift the flour and confectioners' sugar together into a bowl, add the cream, a little at a time, while stirring to blend well. Beat the egg whites into firm, snowy peaks, sift over the superfine sugar and beat into a light, glossy meringue. Tip part of the egg whites onto the main mixture and beat well to lighten it, then carefully fold in the rest of the egg whites. Spoon the mixture into a pastry bag fitted with a ½-inch plain nozzle. Pipe out finger shapes about 2½ inches long on a greased and floured baking sheet about 1 inch apart. They spread and flatten as they bake. Bake until the edges of the cookies are golden colored. Transfer immediately to a wire rack to cool. Store in an airtight container.

MACAROONS

These small, familiar cookies are a good accompaniment to puddings and creams, as well as a sweet mouthful with a cup of coffee or tea or a glass of white wine. Here is a classic recipe using almonds.

MAKES 15 COOKIES

1 cup almonds, toasted and ground	2 teaspoons orange-flower water or brandy
½ cup superfine sugar	1 large egg white
1 drop of vanilla extract or 1 inch vanilla pod, scraped	granulated sugar

425°F: 8–10 minutes.

The method is very simple, but it is essential to beat the paste very thoroughly. Combine the almonds, sugar, vanilla or scraped vanilla seeds and orange-flower water or brandy in a bowl. Mix well. Beat in a little egg white at a time. Work until the paste is slightly soft but not runny.

Not all the egg white may be needed, but if the ground almonds are especially dry, it may be necessary to add a little more. Work well until the mixture is very smooth.

Pinch off olive-size pieces and roll into smooth balls. Space them about 1½ inches apart on a flat baking sheet lined with rice or parchment paper. Slightly flatten each macaroon, then brush with cold water and sprinkle over a little granulated sugar. You may also pipe the past through a large plain nozzle and finish as above.

Bake the macaroons immediately until risen and lightly colored. Transfer them to a wire rack to cool, then store in an airtight container.

VARIATION

Use raw ground almonds and add 2 teaspoons ground cinnamon to the sugar in the basic paste.

ALMOND FLORENTINES

These small, crisp pastries with a toffee and almond topping are quite irresistible.

MAKES 60 PIECES

Pastry

scant ¾ cup flour, sifted

small pinch of salt

4 tablespoons butter, chilled and cubed

1 tablespoon superfine sugar

1 egg yolk

1 tablespoon ice water

Filling

3 tablespoons clear honey

7 tablespoons unsalted butter

½ cup granulated sugar

1 cup slivered almonds

To finish

3 tablespoons apricot jam, warmed and strained

400°F: 20 minutes.

Prepare the pastry as described on p. 14. Wrap and chill for 30 minutes. Meanwhile gently heat the honey, butter, and sugar in a heavy pan until the butter has melted and the sugar has dissolved. Remove the pan from the heat and stir in the almonds, making sure that they are well coated with the mixture. Set aside to cool.

Roll out the pastry on a lightly floured work surface to fit into a 12-by-8-inch lightly greased jelly roll pan. Prick the pastry all over with a fork and parbake for 10 minutes, or until set (see p. 15).

Lift the tray out of the oven, leave the oven on at the same temperature, and brush the pastry with apricot jam. Spread the cooled almond filling evenly all over the apricot surface and replace the tray in the oven to bake for 10 minutes more.

The nut filling will start to brown and bubble slightly. Remove the tray from the oven and immediately cut into 1¼-inch-square florentines, before the mixture sets into a slightly sticky and toffeelike texture. Leave in the pan to cool on a wire rack. The cookies stay fresh for up to 3 weeks if stored in an airtight container.

Florentines may also be served with coffee after dinner, or to accompany an ice-cream dessert.

VINEGAR CAKE WITH FRUITS

Vinegar and brown sugar make this cake moist and very tasty.

2 cups flour

½ teaspoon salt

10 tablespoons butter, cubed

scant 1 cup soft dark-brown sugar

4 tablespoons mixed citrus peel, chopped

½ cup currants

½ cup sultanas

1½ teaspoons baking soda

1 cup milk

1½ tablespoons white vinegar or white wine vinegar

350°F: 1 hour, then 325°F: 20–25 minutes.

Butter an 8-inch loose-bottomed round cake pan. Sift the flour and salt together twice and then into a large mixing bowl. Drop in the butter pieces and lightly blend and rub to a crumb texture. Stir in the sugar, citrus peel, currants, and sultanas.

Dissolve the baking soda in ¼ cup of the milk and mix it into the dry ingredients. Stir the vinegar into the remaining milk and combine it well with the main mixture.

Pour into the prepared cake pan and bake for 1 hour at the higher temperature. Reduce the heat and bake until a skewer comes out dry. Turn out the cake and let cool on a wire rack.

BROWN AND WHITE DUTCH COOKIES

These amusing and decorative cookies are fun to make and add an unusual touch to the coffee table. Try different shapes and combinations. They can be stored in an airtight container for up to 2 weeks.

MAKES 40–50 COOKIES

7 ounces butter, softened	pinch of salt
1 cup confectioners' sugar, sifted	1 inch vanilla pod, scraped
1¼ cups flour, sifted	1 tablespoon cocoa powder
⅓ cup ground almonds	

400°F: 15 minutes.

Cream the butter and sugar until light and fluffy. Add the flour, almonds, salt, and vanilla seeds. Combine and knead into a rough paste. Divide the dough into two parts.

Sprinkle the cocoa powder over 1 portion of paste and gently knead it in until the texture is smooth and the cocoa well distributed. Roll into a long rope and set aside. Finish kneading the remaining paste and roll as above. Wrap both and leave to rest and chill in a cool place for 1 hour.

The cookies may be finished in a variety of ways.

Pinwheels
Roll out both pieces of pastry into two rectangles about ¼ inch thick and measuring approximately 10 by 8 inches. Lay the chocolate-pastry rectangle on top of the plain pastry and, using the rolling pin, gently press both layers together. Cut in half lengthwise into two long strips. Starting from the long side, carefully roll each strip into a long, smooth rope shape about 1 inch in diameter. Wrap and chill again. Cut into ¼-inch slices and space 1 inch apart on a buttered and floured baking sheet. Bake until risen and golden. Cool the pastries on a wire rack.

Chocolate Pipe
Roll out the chilled plain pastry into a rectangle as above. Cut in half lengthwise. Shape the piece of chocolate pastry into two long ropes the same length as the plain pastry and about 1 inch in diameter. Lay one rope on each plain rectangle and carefully wrap the pastry around to enclose the rope. Place, seam side down, on a small wooden board, cover, and chill again. Cut into slices, as above. Finish and bake in the same way.

Vanilla Pipe
Repeat as above, only in reverse—using the chocolate dough for the outside and vanilla dough for the inside.

AMERICAN SOUR CREAM AND SPICED COFFEE CAKE

America is a nation of coffee drinkers, and coffee cakes are featured frequently in American cookbooks. Often they are yeasted and contain dried fruits and spices. This recipe contains many spices, as well as sour cream which gives the cake an almost yeasty taste.

SERVES 4–6

1¾ cups flour	¼ pound butter, softened
pinch of salt	1½ cups soft brown sugar
1 teaspoon baking soda	3 eggs, separated
2 teaspoons ground cinnamon	1¼ cups sour cream
1 teaspoon ground cloves	
½ teaspoon ground nutmeg	

350°F: 1 hour.

Carefully sift the flour, salt, baking soda, cinnamon, cloves, and nutmeg together three times. Set aside. Cream together the butter and sugar until light and fluffy. Lightly beat the egg yolks in a separate bowl, then beat a little at a time into the butter and sugar mixture.

Thoroughly beat alternating spoonfuls of the flour-spice mixture and the sour cream into the butter-sugar-egg mixture. Beat the egg whites until they stand in stiff peaks, then fold them into the mixture, taking care not to lose any air.

Line the bottom of a 9-inch square baking pan or a 9½-inch springform pan with parchment paper, then grease with butter. Pour in the batter, smooth the surface, and bake until risen and golden. Leave in the tin for 10 minutes before turning out to cool on a wire rack.

BAKED CHEESECAKE WITH DRIED FRUITS

MAKES 16 SQUARES

Pastry

⅔ cup flour	¼ cup superfine sugar
¼ cup potato flour or corn flour	zest of 1 lemon
½ teaspoon baking powder	generous 1 cup sour cream
6 tablespoons butter, softened	pinch of ground nutmeg
¼ cup confectioners' sugar	2 tablespoons mixed candied orange and lemon peel, chopped small
pinch of ground nutmeg	6 tablespoons raisins
3 eggs, separated	**To finish**
Filling	confectioners' sugar
1 cup cottage cheese	

400°F: 10 minutes, then 350°F: 40–45 minutes.

To make the pastry, sift the flour, potato flour or corn flour, and baking powder twice and then into a mixing bowl. Cut in the butter and rub it lightly to make a coarse crumb mixture. Sift in the confectioners' sugar and nutmeg and stir to combine. Add part of 1 egg yolk to lightly bind the mixture; use a knife. Lightly knead by hand to blend as described on p. 14.

Roll out the pastry on a floured work surface to fit the bottom of a buttered 8-inch square cake pan. Lift it into the pan, cover with a sheet of wax paper, and weigh down with a few pebbles or beans. Bake blind (see p. 14) for about 10 minutes, or until the pastry has set and colored slightly. Remove the paper and pebbles. Reduce the oven temperature as indicated above.

To make the filling, drop the cottage cheese, sugar, and lemon zest into a bowl and combine well by hand.

Lightly whisk the remaining egg yolks and fold them into the mixture along with the sour cream and nutmeg. In a separate bowl, beat the egg whites into stiff peaks, pour this onto the cheese mixture, and fold it in carefully using a large metal spoon.

Scatter the mixed peel and raisins on the pastry base and pour over the cheese mixture. Bake until risen and golden. Remove from the oven and allow to cool in the pan set on a wire rack. The cheese top has a tendency to crack as it cools, which is part of its charm. Turn out onto a rack to cool thoroughly, then cut into 16 squares. Serve sprinkled with a little confectioners' sugar. Cheesecake keeps fresh for 3–4 days.

MADEIRA CAKE

Here is a very plain, traditional cake that used to be served with a glass of Madeira wine.

MAKES 12 SLICES

7 tablespoons butter, softened	pinch of salt
1/2 cup superfine sugar	4 eggs, lightly beaten
scant 1 1/2 cups flour	1 teaspoon lemon juice
1 teaspoon baking soda	1 teaspoon lemon zest
1 teaspoon cream of tartar	**To decorate**
	3 strips of candied citron peel

350°F: 1–1 1/4 hours.

Beat the butter and sugar together until light and fluffy. Sift the flour, baking soda, cream of tartar, and salt together three times. Sift about a third of the dried ingredients over the butter and sugar mixture. Beat them in well, then blend in a little egg, and half the lemon juice and zest. Add the remaining ingredients in two further parts, beating well between each addition to make a smooth and creamy mixture.

Line and butter the bottom of a 7-inch round cake pan. Pour in the mixture and level the top. Bake in the preheated oven. After about 45 minutes, open the oven door with care and lay the citron pieces at random on the cake top. Bake until well risen, golden, and slightly shrinking from the sides. Test with a skewer for readiness. Leave in the pan for 10 minutes before turning out onto a wire rack to cool.

SPLITTERKUCHEN

SPLINTER CAKE

This cake rises and puffs into split layers, very much like puff pastry.

MAKES 40 SLICES

3/4 cup flour, sifted	1 egg white, lightly beaten
pinch of salt	about 1/2 cup confectioners' sugar, sifted
7 tablespoons butter, softened and cubed	
1/2 cup heavy cream	

400°F: 20 minutes.

Sift the flour and salt into a mixing bowl. Drop in the butter pieces and lightly rub together. Add the cream and, using a blunt kitchen knife or spatula, quickly combine the ingredients into a smooth pastry. Finish by hand. Turn out of the bowl onto a floured work surface and roll out the dough to about 1/2 inch thickness.

Fold up the dough into a 4-inch square and roll out again as before. Repeat the folding and rolling process once more. Wrap in plastic and chill for at least 1 hour.

Roll out the pastry again into a rectangle about 1/4 inch thick and brush all over with the egg white. Dredge heavily with the confectioners' sugar and cut into rectangles about 1 by 3 inches. Place on a lightly greased baking sheet spaced 1/2 inch apart and bake until golden.

Potato Flour Sponge

Potato flour gives this sponge a very light, creamy taste. It is delicate and close-textured and will keep up to a week when stored in an airtight container.

MAKES 36 PIECES

4 egg yolks

¾ cup superfine sugar

2 teaspoons lemon zest

juice of ½ lemon

3 egg whites

⅔ cup potato flour, sifted

6 tablespoons apricot jam, warmed and sieved

To finish

1 recipe lemon glacé icing (p. 18)

300°F: 1 hour 10 minutes

Grease an 8-inch square cake pan with butter, and dust well with sifted potato flour. Beat the egg yolks and sugar together until very pale and creamy. Add the lemon zest and juice and continue beating for a further 10 minutes or so; when the lemon is added, the mixture is quite thin at first but thickens up well and expands even further.

Beat the egg whites until they hold firm peaks, tip them onto the main cake mixture, and gently fold in. Sift over the potato flour and fold that in carefully as well. Pour the batter into the prepared cake pan, rap it smartly on the work top once to burst any bubbles of air, and bake immediately.

When the cake has risen well and slightly colored, remove it from the oven and allow to cool in the pan overnight on a wire rack. Carefully slice the cake into two layers and spread half the apricot jam on the bottom layer. Cover with the top layer. Brush the rest of the jam all over the top and sides.

Prepare the lemon icing and immediately pour over the top, smoothing the remainder on the sides of the cake. Serve cut into squares.

Kaiser Bread with Almonds

MAKES 1 LOAF

¾ cup slivered blanched almonds

2 tablespoons granulated sugar

5 egg yolks

½ cup superfine sugar

3 egg whites

scant ¾ cup flour, sifted

350°F: 1 hour.

Toss the almonds and granulated sugar together in a small heavy pan, then stir over low heat until the sugar has caramelized and the almonds are well coated. Allow to cool on an oiled baking sheet, then separate them.

Beat the egg yolks and superfine sugar in a large bowl until pale and creamy. In another bowl, beat the egg whites until they hold stiff peaks and lightly fold them into the yolk mixture, alternating with spoonfuls of caramelized almonds and sifted flour. Turn the mixture into a buttered balmoral (p. 13) or 1-pound loaf pan and bake until risen and golden. Leave to cool on a wire rack and serve cut into slices.

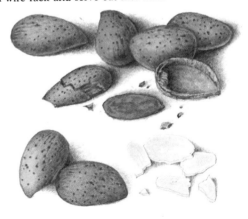

3

AFTERNOON TEA
& HIGH TEA

Tea was first introduced to Britain in the seventeenth century and one hundred years later was the universal beverage for all classes of society, despite the high cost. Tea was offered in the afternoon in fashionable homes and served handsomely from the new china tea services. The elaborate "équipage," as it was known, was sufficient to serve coffee and tea for at least twelve people. Around the beginning of the nineteenth century it became fashionable to offer bread, butter, and cakes along with the beverages.

In Britain delicate sandwiches were served filled with a variety of savories such as cold meats, pastes of fish and meat, egg, cucumber, and tomato and were elegantly laid out on doily-covered silver platters. The cakes were presented on ornate tiered cake stands.

Gradually the light repast developed into a much more substantial affair offering hot toast, crumpets, and teacakes followed by the usual sandwiches, tea breads, butter and jam, numerous cakes, and fruit pies. The cakes were plain—sponge, slab fruitcakes, and ginger cake being typical. The custom of taking an afternoon drink became popular in central Europe,

too, with coffee as the main beverage, but the cakes and pastries that were offered were much more elaborate—gugelhupf, tea breads and doughnuts, streuselkuchen, cheesecakes, and small nut pastries would be served.

Gradually the custom of taking refreshment in the middle of the afternoon spread through all parts of society in Britain, and soon teatime became more important as a meal than as a social occasion. It also became a more homely event, falling in the early evening when work was concluded.

The new meal, known as high tea, was a robust selection of foods combining supper-type dishes with cakes and so avoiding the necessity of a cooked meal later on. Cold meats and pies, salads, sandwich fare, tea breads, and hot muffins and tea cakes were offered, followed by fruit pies, trifle, flavored gelatin, or stewed fruits. Cakes generally tended to be less elaborate; the iced sponges and cream-filled varieties were kept for more special occasions.

Traditions in Europe were much the same as in Britain. The new mealtime, especially among farming communities, fitted well into the daily routine, and

although the food was very similar, the sweet course, often consisting of a "*Mehlspeise*," was especially important. (In Teutonic Europe, Mehlspeise, a floury dessert, had been popular for some centuries and was composed mainly of flour and eggs, butter and milk; sugar was added later. There were even cooks who specialized in this type of cooking.)

By the early part of the twentieth century a whole range of continental confectionery made with unfamiliar baking ingredients was introduced to the British pastry cook; rich chocolate cakes and nut cakes, gugelhupf and strudel, petit fours from France, meringues and éclairs filled with crème pâtissière, and macaroons made with almonds. High tea had become a very elaborate affair. But more recently habits have changed again, and the rich gâteaux and Torten of Europe are now a feature of the elegant dinner table, and teatime has reverted to its original simplicity.

LARDY CAKE

Here is an English specialty, long forgotten, but now becoming popular again. A yeasted-enriched bread dough is rolled and folded, much in the same way as puff pastry, then filled with an irresistible and sticky combination of brown sugar, lard, spice, and dried fruits and peels.

This recipe can also be made easily with quick-rising yeast, if that is available in your supermarket. Follow the directions on the package; the granules will be added directly to the dry flour, not premixed with the warm liquid.

All the ingredients should be warmed to room temperature before starting to bake.

Bread dough

2¼ cups bread flour, sifted

1 teaspoon salt

1½ teaspoons lard

2 packages dry yeast (½ ounce)

¾ cup milk, warmed to 80°F

Filling

generous ½ cup lard, well chilled and cut into small cubes

generous ½ cup soft light-brown sugar

1 teaspoon mixed ground spice

¾ cup mixed fruit and peel, chopped small

To finish

a little beaten egg and milk

granulated sugar

425°F: 30–40 minutes.

Sprinkle the yeast on top of the warmed milk and stir to dissolve. Add a pinch of sugar, stir, and set in a warm place until it becomes foamy and about doubled in bulk.

Sift the flour and salt together into a large bowl. Cut in the lard and rub together to blend, then stir in the yeast mixture; begin kneading immediately in the bowl.

When the dough starts to roll off the sides of the bowl, turn it out onto a floured work surface and knead hard for about 10 minutes, or until it feels elastic, is shiny, and large pockets of air are forming.

Roll the dough into a ball, place it in the mixing bowl, cover with a floured cloth, and set aside in a warm place to rise and double in bulk. This may take 1–2 hours.

Flour the work surface and roll out the risen dough into a rectangle just less than ¼ inch thick. Dot one-third of the lard across the surface to within ½ inch of the edges and scatter over a third each of the sugar, the spice, the mixed fruit and peel.

Fold one-third of the dough over from the short side into the middle and cover it by folding the rest of the dough on top. Firmly press the edges together so that the filling is completely sealed in. Swing the dough a quarter turn to the right and indent with two fingers on the lower short side. Cover and chill in the refrigerator for 15 minutes.

Roll, as before, from the indented side into a rectangle ¼ inch thick. Dot with half the remaining ingredients, fold, seal, turn again, indent, and chill.

Repeat the rolling, filling, and folding procedures with the rest of the ingredients. Finally roll and fold the dough to fit snugly into an 8-inch greased square cake pan. Press down well into the corners. Cover the pan with the floured cloth and leave for at least 30 minutes, or until the dough has risen again and doubled in bulk.

Before setting the risen dough in the preheated oven, brush the surface with a little beaten egg and milk and sprinkle generously with granulated sugar. With a sharp knife, score a crisscross pattern across the surface from one side to the other, cutting in about ⅛ inch. Bake until well risen and golden. Allow to cool, upside down, on a wire rack.

Cut into slices and serve while still warm, or cold if you prefer. As with all yeasted recipes, lardy cake tastes best on the day of baking.

LEMON CAKE

Here is the simplest of lemon cakes, with a crunchy taste and a sharp tang. Although it is similar to a pound cake (p. 20), the lemon syrup that is poured over while it is still hot totally changes the texture and character of the cake.

½ cup superfine sugar	2 teaspoons lemon zest
7 tablespoons butter, softened	2 tablespoons warm water
2 eggs	scant ⅓ cup granulated sugar
scant ¾ cup flour	
½ teaspoon baking powder	juice of 1 lemon

350°F: 1 hour.

Beat the sugar and butter together until pale and fluffy. Beat in the eggs, one at a time. Sift the flour and baking powder together twice, then sift and combine one-third with the mixture, taking care not to over-beat. Fold in the second third, and when that is beaten in, add the remainder. Finally mix in the lemon zest and the warm water. Pour into a buttered 1-pound loaf pan and bake immediately in the preheated oven.

Make the syrup meanwhile by gently dissolving the granulated sugar in the lemon juice over a gentle heat.

Lift the cake out of the oven when it has browned and started to shrink away from the sides of the pan. Turn it upside down onto a wire rack with a serving plate set underneath.

Prick the cake all over with a fork and carefully spoon over two-thirds of the lemon syrup. Turn the cake right side up, prick again, and spoon the remaining juices over it. Remember to use the juice on the plate as well. When all the liquid is absorbed, allow the cake to cool. Lemon cake keeps fresh for several days wrapped and in an airtight container.

BATTENBERG

This cake is made of colored layers of Genoese sponge sandwiched with jam and wrapped in marzipan. The derivation of the name is unknown, although Battenberg does have royal connections in Britain. Princess Beatrice, one of Queen Victoria's daughters, married a German princeling, Henry of Battenberg, and later the name was anglicized to Mountbatten. Perhaps this cake was prepared for their wedding celebrations. Battenberg keeps fresh for up to 1 week.

2 teaspoons instant coffee powder or granules	6 ounces unsalted butter, melted and cooled
1 teaspoon boiling water	½ cup apricot jam, warmed and strained
6 eggs, separated	
scant 1 cup superfine sugar	**To finish**
scant 1¼ cups flour, sifted	1 pound marzipan (p. 86)
2 inches vanilla pod, split	glacé fruits

350°F: 45 minutes.

Prepare a deep, 8-inch-square cake pan. Divide the pan in half with a piece of foil by lining the base of the pan and making a deep pleat in the center, the height of the pan. Insert a piece of cardboard in the pleat to support it. Brush all over with melted butter. Dissolve the coffee powder or granules in the boiling water and set aside to cool. Prepare the Genoese sponge with the eggs, sugar, flour, and vanilla, using the cold method with separated egg whites described on p. 15. Fold the melted butter in to finish. Spoon half the batter into one side of the prepared tin.

Lightly fold the coffee into the remaining cake batter and spoon it into the other side of the cake pan. Gently level both surfaces, rap the pan once to dispel any air bubbles, and bake. After the cakes have settled for 10 minutes, turn out of the pan to cool on a wire rack. Leave overnight.

Prepare the marzipan as described on p. 87.

Next day, trim both cakes neatly and divide in half lengthwise. Sandwich the four pieces together, alternating the flavors, with half the apricot jam. Cut a sheet of parchment paper to exactly the length of the cake and wide enough to go around it, leaving the ends bare.

Roll out the marzipan on top of it just to fit. Brush the marzipan surface with the remaining apricot jam, lay the assembled cake across the middle, and, using the paper as a guide, carefully wrap the marzipan around the Battenberg. Smooth out any indentations before removing the paper. Sharply pinch together the two joined edges and inch the other top edge to match. Decorate with glacé fruits of your choice.

AUSTRIAN CHEESECAKE

Baked cheesecakes are very popular in central Europe. Topfen, the Austrian curd cheese, features in many sweet combinations, either as an integral part of the pastry or as a filling blended with various flavors and ingredients. Baked cheesecakes generally rise and puff high as they bake, then collapse dramatically and crack as they cool. The texture of the cake remains smooth and moist. The version of cheesecake most familiar in Britain and America today, blended and stiffened with gelatin, has never been part of European cuisine. It is of American origin, quite different in character from the baked ones, and more suitable as a dessert (see p. 69).

7 tablespoons butter, softened	1 teaspoon lemon zest
½ cup superfine sugar	1 cup slivered almonds
4 eggs, separated	**To finish**
¼ cup cottage cheese, sieved	confectioners' sugar or sour cream

350°F: 45 minutes.

Beat the butter and sugar together until light and fluffy. Beat in one egg yolk at a time until well blended, then add the cottage cheese and lemon zest. Mix in the almonds. In a separate bowl, beat the egg whites into firm and creamy peaks. Blend about one-third into the main batter to lighten it, then carefully fold in the rest of the egg whites.

   Have ready a 9½-inch springform cake pan buttered and dusted with flour, pour in the cake batter, level the top a little, then sharply rap the pan on the work surface to burst any pockets of air. Bake immediately until puffed and golden. Test with a skewer, then leave in the pan to cool on a wire rack. Serve the cheesecake sprinkled with confectioners' sugar; or spread a layer of sour cream over the top.

CHOCOLATE HEDGEHOG CAKE

This is a most attractive, light-textured cake with spikes of almond flakes in the chocolate icing to resemble hedgehog spines.

6 tablespoons butter, softened	scant ⅔ cup potato flour, sifted
scant ⅔ cup superfine sugar	**To decorate**
4½ ounces plain dark chocolate, melted and cooled (p. 11)	¼ cup apricot jam
	chocolate icing (p. 19)
6 egg whites	¾ cup slivered almonds, toasted

325°F: 1 hour approximately.

Beat the butter and ½ cup of the sugar until light and fluffy. Mix in the chocolate until well blended. Beat the egg whites in a separate bowl until they hold firm, creamy peaks; sift over the reserved sugar and beat until the mixture is shiny and smooth.

   Beat 2 tablespoons of egg white into the chocolate mixture to lighten it, then tip on the rest and lightly fold it in, along with the potato flour. Pour the mixture into a buttered and floured 12-inch balmoral pan (p. 13), lightly smooth the surface, and bake until risen and lightly shrinking from the sides of the pan. Allow the cake to cool on a wire rack. Warm the apricot jam with 1 tablespoon water, strain, and brush all over the cake. Prepare the chocolate icing and immediately pour it over. Stud the toasted slivered almonds in the chocolate before it starts to set, to resemble the spines of a hedgehog.

SWITZEN PLUM

Kenneth F. Laidlaw

Streuselkuchen

Yeasted doughs are a popular central European confectionery. They are not the simple bread doughs that we generally find in Britain, but are enriched, often lavishly, with butter and eggs and flavored with nuts and dried fruits. Fruited gugelhupf and Viennese kipfel stuffed with nuts, and peasant breads for festivities, barely able to support an extravagance of dried fruits, are common.

A simple but rich basic dough such as this one acts as a foundation for various toppings. It may be layered and filled with crème pâtissière or covered with a caramelized sugar, butter, and almond layer known as bee sting, or bienenstich. But most popular are the crumb-topped streuselkuchen and the layered fruit versions that follow.

MAKES 24 SLICES

Yeast dough	
½ cup milk, warmed to 80°F	*a little melted butter*
1¾ cups bread flour	**Streusel or crumb topping**
¾ ounce fresh yeast or 1½ teaspoons dried yeast	*1 cup flour*
2 tablespoons superfine sugar	*pinch of ground cinnamon*
pinch of salt	*1 teaspoon lemon zest*
4 egg yolks, lightly beaten	*scant ½ cup superfine sugar*
4 tablespoons unsalted butter, softened	*¼ pound unsalted butter, chilled*
	¾ cup slivered almonds

375°F: 25–30 minutes

Make a yeast sponge batter, as described on p. 16 with the milk, ⅔ cup of the flour, the yeast, and 1 teaspoon of the sugar. Set aside to rise. Sift the remaining flour, salt, and sugar twice and then into a bowl. Mix in the yeast batter and combine; mix in the egg yolks and butter.

Beat and knead well. Continue kneading thoroughly until the dough is shiny and elastic and starts to throw large bubbles of air. Cover the bowl with a floured cloth and leave to rise in a warm place for 30–40 minutes, or until it has doubled in bulk.

Meanwhile prepare the crumb topping. Sift together the flour and cinnamon; stir in the lemon zest and sugar. Cut in the butter and rub with the flour to a rather coarse and crumbly texture. Drop in the slivered almonds and toss them around well to combine. Cover and chill.

When the yeast dough has risen and doubled in bulk, knock it back and knead for a minute or two longer. Turn it out onto a floured board and roll it out to about ½ inch thick and large enough to fit two 12-by-8-by-1½-inch baking sheets.

Cut the dough in half and lift each piece onto a greased sheet, pressing it gently into place with a floured hand. It will level out as it rises. Leave to rise once more in a warm place for about 20 minutes.

When doubled in bulk, brush the surface with a little melted butter and sprinkle the prepared topping all over the risen dough. Bake in the preheated oven. Remove from the oven when golden and cut while still warm on the baking sheets into rectangular pieces. Leave on the sheets to cool on a wire rack.

Switzen Plums on Yeast Dough

A yeasted dough base is also delicious layered with fresh fruits. Apricots and cherries are good, but most popular and traditional, especially in Germany and Austria, are switzen—Zwetschken—plums. These rich purple fruits with a pale-green-tinged flesh appear in midautumn. Their slightly tart flavor blends well with the rich yeast dough. Do not sugar the fruits before baking, for the juices are drawn out and will soak and spoil the pastry. If you can't get switzen plums, use greengages or cooking plums.

MAKES 12 SLICES

½ recipe yeast dough (see streuselkuchen, p. 43)

2 pounds switzen or greengage plums, halved and pitted

melted butter

⅓ cup ground almonds or ½ cup toasted bread crumbs

1 teaspoon ground cinnamon

To finish

1 teaspoon ground cinnamon

2 tablespoons superfine sugar

375°F: 25–30 minutes.

Prepare the yeast dough as in the previous recipe. Leave to rise, then knead again, roll out, and line a baking sheet. Cover and leave to rise again. Meanwhile prepare the fruit.

When the dough has doubled in bulk, brush with the melted butter, then sprinkle with the almonds or bread crumbs. Pack the fruits onto the dough, cut side up, overlapping them slightly, and sift the cinnamon all over. Bake in the preheated oven until the dough is well risen and golden at the edges. Remove from the oven and cut into rectangles while still hot. Allow

to cool on the sheet on a wire rack. Dredge with sugar and cinnamon before serving.

BLITZKUCHEN

A popular German classic, this cake has a pleasant nutty filling that contrasts well with the lemon icing.

¾ cup superfine sugar

4 eggs

¾ cup flour, sifted

6 tablespoons butter, melted and cooled

Filling

¾ cup ground almonds or hazelnuts

scant ½ cup superfine sugar

1 inch vanilla pod, split

milk or cream

2 tablespoons apricot jam, warmed and strained

To decorate

lemon glacé icing (p. 18)

glacé fruits

350°F: 35 minutes.

Beat the sugar with 1 whole egg and 3 yolks until light and very fluffy. Sift over the flour and blend in carefully. Beat the remaining egg whites in a separate bowl into firm and creamy peaks and gently fold them into the egg mixture, trying not to lose any beaten-in air. Carefully fold in the melted butter.

Pour into a buttered 9½-inch springform pan and bake immediately in the preheated oven until risen and golden. Leave in the pan set on a wire rack for 15 minutes. Turn out and allow to cool overnight.

Filling: combine the first three ingredients in a bowl. Stir in a small amount of milk or cream at a time until a spreading consistency is reached. Slice the cake into two layers and spread the filling over the bottom layer; sandwich with the top layer. Seal the top with a coating of warmed and strained apricot jam. Prepare the lemon icing and pour it over the cake. Decorate with glacé fruits.

CHOCOLATE BREAD

This bread has a good moist texture and a rich, spicy flavor.

4 eggs	1 teaspoon lemon zest
scant 1 cup superfine sugar	½ teaspoon ground cinnamon
1 cup slivered blanched almonds (optional)	pinch of ground nutmeg
6 tablespoons chopped candied orange and lemon peel	1 teaspoon baking powder
	scant 1½ cups flour, sifted
4½ ounces plain dark chocolate, melted and cooled (p. 11)	

350°F: 1 hour.

Beat the eggs and sugar together until pale and fluffy, mix in the almonds (if used), chopped peels, melted chocolate, and lemon zest. Sift the spices and baking powder together with the flour and mix a spoonful at a time into the main mixture. It is important not to overbeat.

Pour into a buttered 1-pound loaf pan and bake in the preheated oven. Test the bread with a skewer for readiness; it should come out dry. Leave it in the pan for 10 minutes before turning out onto a wire rack to cool.

BRAN TEA BREAD

1 cup bran	1¼ cups milk
1½ cups sultanas	2 tablespoons rum
1⅓ cups soft light-brown sugar	scant 1¼ cups flour
	1 teaspoon baking powder

375°F: 1–1¼ hours.

Combine the cereal, sultanas, sugar, milk, and rum in a bowl and leave to soak overnight. Prepare a 1-pound loaf pan by lining the base with parchment paper and greasing all over with butter.

Sift the flour and baking powder together twice, then sift half onto the bran mixture and blend in well; sift over and mix in the rest of the flour. Pour into the pan and bake immediately. Turn out of the pan, strip off the papers, and leave to cool on a wire rack. Serve sliced and spread with butter.

GÂTEAU PITHIVIERS

This well-known rum and marzipan puff pastry originates in the French town of Pithiviers, not far from
Paris. Although it takes some time to prepare, it can
be assembled without the decoration well ahead of time
and frozen, uncooked, without harm, for up to 2 months.
Make the marzipan a day ahead if possible so that it
is well chilled and firm before use. Serve Pithiviers as
a special teatime treat. It is best eaten while still warm.

1 pound puff pastry dough, fresh or frozen	4 tablespoons butter, softened
1 egg, lightly beaten	1 egg yolk, lightly beaten
Marzipan	2 tablespoons dark rum
½ cup ground almonds	**To finish**
scant ½ cup superfine sugar	confectioners' sugar

450°F: 15 minutes, then 400°F: 30–40 minutes.

Make the marzipan first. Combine the almonds, sugar,
butter, and egg yolk in a bowl and beat to a smooth
paste. Blend in the rum. Roll into a ball, wrap, and
chill until firm.

The puff pastry dough should be well chilled but
not frozen when it is used. Cut off about one-third of
the dough and leave the rest wrapped in the refrigerator. Roll the piece on a floured work surface into
an 8½-inch circle, trimming a sharp edge with the
point of a knife; this encourages the puffed layers to
separate and rise properly during baking. Transfer the
pastry circle to a wet baking sheet. Cover and chill
for 30 minutes.

Work the cold marzipan for a moment to soften
it, then press it onto the pastry to within 1 inch of
the edge. Brush cold water around the pastry edge.

Roll out the reserved puff pastry to a circle of the
same size and about twice the thickness of the base

and cut a sharp edge again. Lay the pastry circle on
top of the almond layer and firmly press together the
two pastry edges to form a tight seal. Cut out a scalloped border with the tip of a sharp knife dipped in
hot water. Cover and chill for 30 minutes more.

Make a small chimney to allow the steam from the
cooking marzipan to escape: form a hollow tube of foil
about ½ inch in diameter and 2 inches long. Butter
it well. Brush the pastry top with some of the egg and
cut a hole in the center to insert the chimney. Brush
over a second coating of egg.

Using the tip of a sharp, pointed knife, cut the
traditional Pithiviers pattern about ⅛ inch into the
puff pastry. Starting from the center, the lines are
incised in a half-moon curve to the scalloped border.

Prick right through the pastry to the baking sheet
in about six places and bake immediately in the preheated oven as instructed. Dredge a generous layer of
confectioners' sugar over the cake 10 minutes before
the cooking time is completed, then finish baking. The
pastry will have risen high and have a lightly caramelized, golden surface. Remove the chimney and allow to cool on a wire rack. Serve lukewarm if possible.

PECAN PIE

Pecans are indigenous to the United States and are now becoming popular in Britain. The nut slightly resembles a walnut when removed from its shell, but the flavor is different and quite distinctive.

Sweet shortcrust pastry

scant 1¼ cups flour, sifted

pinch of salt

¼ pound butter, chilled and cubed

¼ cup superfine sugar

1 egg, lightly beaten

2 tablespoons ice water

Filling

¾ cup golden syrup

about ½ cup light-brown sugar

3 eggs, lightly beaten

4 tablespoons unsalted butter, melted and cooled

½ teaspoon lemon zest

pinch of salt

1 tablespoon dark rum

about 2 cups pecans

400°F: 20 minutes, then 350°F: 40 minutes.

Prepare the pastry with the dough as described on p. 14 and chill. Line a 9-inch flan tin with the dough. Notch a pattern around the edge and prick all over with a fork. Lay a sheet of wax paper on top and weigh down with beans or pebbles. Bake blind (p. 14) for 10 minutes at 400°F, then reduce the heat to 350°F for 15–20 minutes more, or until the pastry is slightly colored. Allow to cool while making the filling. Raise the oven temperature.

In a bowl combine the syrup, sugar, eggs, butter, lemon zest, salt, and rum. Stir in the pecans. Pour the filling into the cooled pastry shell and bake at the higher temperature for 20 minutes, then reduce the heat and bake until risen and golden. Allow to cool in the tin, set on a wire rack. Serve lukewarm or cold with rum-flavored whipped cream on the side.

TREACLE TART

An English teatime treat. It is customary to make the tart in an enameled, shallow pie plate. Take care to cut a double edge of pastry for the border.

Sweet shortcrust pastry

scant 1¼ cups flour

pinch of salt

¼ pound butter, chilled

2 tablespoons superfine sugar

1 egg, lightly beaten

2 tablespoons ice water

Filling

1 teaspoon lemon zest

scant ½ cup rolled oats

¼ teaspoon ground ginger

1 cup golden syrup

2 tablespoons lemon juice

400°F: 30 minutes.

Prepare the pastry as described on p. 14 and chill for 30 minutes. Roll the dough out a little larger than the size of a 9-inch pie plate. Reserve the scraps. Let the dough relax for a few minutes before proceeding. Cut off the extra pastry and the dampened edge of the plate with a strip ½ inch wide. Lightly brush it with water.

Carefully lift the pastry circle onto the plate and press the 2 layers together. Mix the rolled oats, lemon zest, and ginger and sprinkle half the mixture over the tart base. Pour on the syrup and lemon juice and finish with the rest of the oats mixture.

Roll out the remaining strip of pastry thinly, cut into ½-inch-wide strips, twist them, and lay them in trellis fashion on the tart surface. Cut small floral trims to decorate the sides. Bake and serve hot or cold.

Carrot and Almond Cake

Carrots are an unusual ingredient here and give a pleasant moisture and fine color to the cake. Almonds, too, in their brown skins, have a special taste that combines well with the carrots. The cake should be stored undecorated and well wrapped for 2 days before being finished and cut, so that the flavors and texture may develop and mature to their best advantage.

about 3 medium-size carrots	*pinch of ground cloves*
4 eggs, separated	**To finish**
1 cup superfine sugar	*3 tablespoons apricot*
1½ cups unblanched almonds, coarsely ground	*jam, warmed and strained*
1 tablespoon dark rum	*1 recipe lemon glacé icing (p. 18)*
1 tablespoon lemon zest	*orange marzipan carrots*
2 tablespoons potato flour	*slivered almonds, toasted*
1 teaspoon baking powder	
1 teaspoon ground cinnamon	

350°F: 50 minutes.

Peel the carrots, grate them finely, and leave in a colander to drain. Beat the egg yolks and sugar together into a creamy foam. Add the well-drained strained carrots, the almonds, rum, and lemon zest. Blend together well. Sift together the potato flour, baking powder, cinnamon, and cloves and lightly combine a spoonful at a time with the main mixture.

Beat the egg whites in a separate bowl into firm, snowy peaks and carefully fold them into the carrot mixture. Have prepared a 9½-inch springform pan, base lined with parchment paper, greased and dusted with a half-and-half mixture of flour and sugar. Pour in the cake batter and bake.

When the cake has risen well and is golden colored, test with a skewer to check that the center has cooked through. Remove from the oven, but leave in the pan for 10 minutes before turning out to cool on a wire rack. Wrap and store for 2 days to mature.

Serve either dredged with confectioners' sugar and whipped cream on the side or decorate as follows:

Brush the top and sides of the cake with apricot jam. Prepare the glacé icing as described on p. 18. Pour it over the cake and decorate immediately with marzipan carrots and slivered toasted almonds.

Almond Cake

Nuts have been used in cooking since early times, not only in sweet pastries but also for thickening savory dishes. Almonds, walnuts, and pistachios, the most coveted, were brought to Europe from the East by the Crusaders, and while fondness for pistachios had waned by the nineteenth century, almonds, walnuts, and hazelnuts too, remained as popular as ever, particularly in central Europe. There, the finest nut pastries and cakes from around the world have been absorbed into the confectioner's repertoire.

The simple almond cake recipe that follows is typical, with its full, rich flavor of almonds, enhanced by a tang of citrus. Nuts are rich in oils, so much so that many recipes exclude butter altogether, and flour is often omitted too. This recipe is quite adaptable. Unblanched ground almonds (which give a more crunchy texture), walnuts, or hazelnuts may be substituted.

All nut cakes taste better after a few days, when the flavors have had time to blend and mature. Store them in an airtight container, undecorated, until needed. This recipe is both quick and easy to prepare; but for a lighter-textured cake, you may prefer to separate the eggs, and fold the whites into the main mixture at the end.

1 1/3 cups superfine sugar	1 recipe lemon glacé icing (p. 18), or chocolate icing (p. 19)
4 eggs	
1 teaspoon lemon zest	
1 1/2 cups ground blanched almonds	**To decorate**
	(optional)
1 tablespoon apricot jam, warmed and strained	a few glacé fruits or nuts

350°F: 1 hour.

Beat the sugar and eggs together until they are pale and foamy. Add the lemon zest. Carefully fold in the almonds to blend well. Turn the mixture into a buttered and floured 9½-inch springform cake pan. Bake until golden and slightly shrinking from the sides of the pan. Allow to settle for a few minutes, then run a sharp knife around the sides of the pan before turning the cake out onto a wire rack.

When the cake has cooled, lightly brush the surface with warmed apricot jam. Prepare the icing and pour it over the top, smoothing a little on the sides. Decorate with a few glacé fruits or nuts if you wish. Serve with whipped cream on the side.

VARIATIONS

Walnut Cake
Walnuts—ground with care so as not to release the bitter oils—may be used instead of almonds. The lemon zest should be omitted, and 2 inches scraped vanilla pod and 1 teaspoon of instant coffee powder dissolved in 1 teaspoon boiling water should be added. Cover the cake with coffee icing (p. 19); decorate with walnut halves and liqueur-filled chocolate coffee beans.

Hazelnut Cake
Hazelnuts, too, taste good. Roast and grind them and flavor the cake with vanilla. Cover it with chocolate icing (p. 19) to make a delicious after-dinner dessert served with whipped cream.

BRANDY SNAPS

MAKES 20 SNAPS

3/4 cup flour	1/2 cup golden syrup
1/2 teaspoon ground ginger	1 tablespoon brandy
1/2 teaspoon ground allspice	**Filling**
7 tablespoons butter, chilled and cubed	2 cups whipped cream
scant 2/3 cup superfine sugar	crystallized fruits

325°F: each batch 6–7 minutes.

The dough may either be used immediately or reserved for a day in the refrigerator to allow the flavors to develop. Bake only 2 or 3 snaps at a time, for they spread to about five times their original size. They should be rolled as soon as they are lifted off the tray, before they harden.

Sift the flour, ginger, and allspice together well to aerate, and then into a bowl. Drop in the butter pieces and rub to a crumb texture. Stir in the sugar, syrup, and brandy and blend to a smooth dough. Roll into a ball. Pinch off walnut-sized pieces and space well apart on a buttered baking sheet. Flatten slightly. Bake with care, for they burn easily. Let cool for a moment or two before sliding each one off the tray and rolling it around a greased wooden spoon handle. Allow to set and harden for a few minutes before transferring to a wire rack to cool.

The snaps keep well when wrapped between layers of wax paper in an airtight container. Serve filled with whipped cream and studded with dried or crystallized fruits.

49

SCONES

These plain, very light cakes originate in Scone in Scotland and in early times were probably cooked on a "girdle," or griddle over a peat fire. They taste best buttered and still warm from the oven, and clotted cream and strawberry jam make them a special treat.

MAKES 10 SCONES

1⅔ cups flour	¼ cup superfine sugar
2½ teaspoons baking powder	1 egg yolk, lightly beaten
	about ⅔ cup milk
pinch of ground nutmeg	**To finish**
5 tablespoons butter, chilled and cubed	beaten egg or a little flour

450°F: 7–10 minutes.

Sift the flour, baking powder, and nutmeg together twice and then into a large bowl. Add the butter pieces and rub to a crumb texture. Stir in the sugar. Make a deep well in the flour; pour in the egg yolk and almost all the liquid. Mix to a soft, spongy dough with a palette knife. Add more milk if necessary. Turn the dough out onto a floured work surface and knead it lightly until it is just smooth. Roll it out to about ½ inch thick and cut out rounds with a 2-inch plain cutter. Place the scones on a greased baking sheet and either brush the tops with beaten egg for a glossy crust or dust with flour for a soft one. Leave to rest for 15 minutes before baking. Remove from the oven when well risen and golden. Serve warm or cold.

SCOTTISH PANCAKES

Another traditional Scottish specialty, these should be cooked on a heavy griddle or a solid electric hot plate. Like scones, they taste best when warm and served with butter.

MAKES 30 PANCAKES

1⅔ cups flour	4 tablespoons butter, cubed
1 tablespoon baking powder	1 egg
pinch of salt	about 1 cup milk
¼ cup superfine sugar or golden syrup	lard for cooking

Sift the flour, baking powder, salt, and sugar, if used, two or three times. Rub in the butter pieces. Mix in the egg and syrup, if used, and about three-quarters of the milk and beat well to form a thick batter. Add more milk if necessary. The batter should settle to its own level.

Have the griddle or hot plate ready, heated to a medium heat. To test for the correct temperature, a hand held ½ inch above the surface should feel comfortably warm. Rub a little lard all over the surface, and when it gives off a light haze, it is ready for use. Drop well-spaced tablespoons of the batter in neat circles on the heated griddle or hot plate. The batter will rise; as bubbles start to break the surface, turn the pancakes over to cook on the underside. Both sides should be golden and should feel slightly spongy. Keep warm wrapped in a tea towel and serve immediately.

CHOCOLATE SACHER TORTE

Mention chocolate cake, and Sacher torte springs immediately to mind. Named after the Sacher family, it is probably the most famous of Austria's extensive and delicious pastry repertoire. The recipe, which is still used at the Sacher pâtisserie in Vienna, is a well-kept secret that late in the nineteenth century became the subject of an acrimonious court case. This recipe may or may not be the authentic one!

6 tablespoons butter, softened	**To decorate**
scant ½ cup superfine sugar	2 tablespoons apricot jam, warmed and strained
3½ ounces of plain dark chocolate, melted and cooled (p. 11)	chocolate icing (p. 19)
4 egg yolks	chocolate scrolls or leaves (optional)
5 egg whites	
½ cup flour, sifted	

325°F: 1¼ hours.

Cream the butter and sugar together until light and fluffy. Beat in the chocolate, then mix in the egg yolks singly, beating well between each. In a separate bowl, beat the egg whites into firm, snowy peaks, then, alternating with spoonfuls of sifted flour, lightly fold them into the chocolate mixture.

Have ready a 9½-inch springform cake pan, buttered and dusted with flour, and pour in the batter. Sharply rap the pan on the work surface to disperse any air bubbles, then bake in the preheated oven.

The cake does not rise very much. Test carefully with a skewer for readiness; it should come out dry. Remove from the oven and, after about 10 minutes, turn out onto a wire rack inverted, so that it cools top side uppermost. When cool, trim the upper side straight and turn the cake over. Brush with the prepared apricot jam.

Prepare the chocolate icing and immediately pour it over the apricot surface. Smooth carefully and allow to set. Traditionally, the cake has no further decoration, though you may prefer to lay a few chocolate scrolls or leaves on top. Serve with lightly sweetened whipped cream on the side.

Sacher Torte improves with keeping and tastes better after 3 or 4 days.

APPLE AND GINGER SLICES

Apples in this mixture give a pleasant, moist texture to the cake.

1 pound cooking apples	6 ounces butter, softened
1 teaspoon lemon juice	generous 1 cup soft light-brown sugar
1 cup flour	3 eggs
1 teaspoon baking powder	
1½ teaspoons ground ginger	1 tablespoon clear honey
½ teaspoon ground cinnamon	4 tablespoons crystallized or stem ginger, chopped small

350°F: 1 hour 10 minutes.

Line the base of a 9½-inch springform pan with parchment paper and butter the base and sides. Peel, core, and slice the apples about ¼ inch thick and sprinkle with lemon juice to prevent discoloration. Sift together the flour, baking powder, ground ginger, and cinnamon. Set aside.

Beat the butter and sugar together until light and fluffy, then mix in the eggs, one at a time, beating well between each addition. If the mixture starts to curdle, add a tablespoon of the flour mixture. Stir in the honey. Blend in the flour mixture a little at a time, without overbeating, until it is well incorporated. Fold in the ginger pieces. Spoon half the batter into the pan, cover with a layer of apple slices, and top with the remaining cake batter. Bake until well risen and springy to the touch. Remove from the oven, but leave in the pan for 10 minutes to settle before turning out to cool.

FRESH ORANGE CAKE

This is an unusual fruit cake, which uses whole fresh oranges; it has a fine, moist texture with a pleasant fragrance. Take care when folding in the egg whites in order to retain as much air as possible to counter the effect of the rather wet and heavy fruits. Choose thin-skinned oranges if they are available, for thicker skins have more white pith and tend to give a slightly bitter taste. The cake keeps no more than 4–5 days.

½ pound oranges	*2 inches vanilla pod, scraped*
4 eggs, separated	
1 cup superfine sugar	*scant ½ cup potato flour or pastry flour, sifted*
¾ cup flour, sifted	
7 ounces butter, melted and cooled	**To finish**
	confectioners' sugar

375°F: 50 minutes.

Wash and dry the oranges carefully. Quarter them, discard the seeds, and mince the rest coarsely. Place in a colander and let drain. Beat the egg yolks and half the sugar together into a pale, creamy froth. Mix in the flour, butter, and vanilla seeds and beat thoroughly.

Discard the drained orange juice and mix the orange mince into the cake batter. Beat the egg whites in a separate bowl until they stand in firm, snowy peaks. Beat the remaining sugar into the egg whites until they are glossy and firm. Tip this over the main mixture and along with siftings of potato flour, fold in

carefully and lightly. The mixture may be rather soft and a little runny; pour it into a buttered and floured 9½-inch springform pan and bake immediately.

When the cake has colored to a dark golden brown, test carefully with a skewer to check that it has cooked through properly; the skewer should come out clean. Remove from the oven, leave in the pan for 10 minutes before turning out onto a wire rack to cool. Serve dredged with confectioners' sugar and whipped cream on the side.

4

AFTER-DINNER DESSERTS

Early in the nineteenth century, French confectionery was influenced by the architectural and sculptural studies of the great master chef Antonin Carême, who prepared all his decorative cakes and table centerpieces like true representations of the applied arts. The ingredients used were of the finest quality, though the finished articles must have posed quite a challenge to those who had to serve them.

Austrian and Hungarian pastries, on the other hand, placed less emphasis on the decorative element and concentrated more on the blending of fine flavors. Cake shapes remained traditionally round and square, and the decorations were simple crystallized fruits and flowers or marzipan fashioned into fruits, figures, leaves, and petals.

By the late nineteenth century the confectionery of France and Austro-Hungary began to make an impact on eating habits in England and America. Until then both nations had been content with plainer fare, but when the refugees from war-stricken Europe offered their traditional and much richer pastries, they were adopted with enthusiasm and quickly assimilated into the cuisine. Continental cake shops flourished.

With a new consciousness of diet and healthy eating, and as the teatime tradition declined in popularity, cakes, particularly the rich continental varieties, fell into disrepute; they became almost forbidden sweetmeats. But it is difficult to resist a new tradition, particularly one that is so tempting. Where better to continue it than at the dinner table? Here is the perfect place for an elaborate indulgence in a public, sympathetic, and excusing environment; "naughty but nice" is the popular phrase.

The layered cakes that follow may be prepared a few days ahead of time and, indeed, improve because their flavors combine and mature. Most may be frozen for 1–2 months (see p. 12). The roulade aux marrons glacés, however, is best made on the day it is to be eaten, when it is at its freshest; for a longer-keeping sponge, substitute the Genoese mixture on p. 16, but fill it at the last moment.

Soft fruit flans are always filled just before they are needed so that the pastry does not get moist, but the empty cooked pastry shells may be kept for 4–5 days if well wrapped in foil or plastic and stored in a cool place. (Avoid freezing them, since they tend to get soggy whey they defrost.)

The filling and pastry for gâteau Saint Honoré may be prepared 1–2 days ahead of time, but the choux crown and final assembly should be left until the day it is needed.

MERINGUES

These are probably the most gratifying confections in the whole sweet repertoire. Composed only of egg white and sugar but optionally garnished with whipped cream, with nuts or chocolate, or with fresh fruits, they present an irresistible temptation to the most determined of dessert abstainers. Baked as small individual meringues or puffed circles to be sandwiched with delectable creams, the basic mixture remains the same in the proportion of 1 egg white to about ⅓ cup superfine sugar.

FOR A 9½-INCH CIRCLE OR 20 SMALL MERINGUES

3 egg whites, at room temperature	1 cup superfine sugar

275°F: 1½–3 hours, depending on size.

Prepare a large baking sheet. Line with parchment paper, and draw on it a circle 9½ inches in diameter if making a flat sheet of meringue. Drop the egg whites into a large copper bowl or spotlessly clean mixing bowl. Beat slowly at first until they begin to froth, then vigorously. The more air that is beaten in the better; lifting the whisk up and through all parts of the mixture in a figure-eight movement as you work gives the best results.

When the egg snow has thickened to a dense mass and soft but firm, creamy peaks have formed, you should be able to invert the bowl without the whites slipping out. Stop beating now.

Dredge over about half the sugar. Continue beating in the same way and incorporate the sugar until the mixture is smooth and glossy. Dredge over the remaining sugar (larger amounts should be folded in in two or three stages), and gently fold it in, using a large metal spoon.

Use a figure-eight movement to retain as much air as possible. Cut down in the mixture, tilt the spoon, and fold over the meringue very lightly, then lift it up and out high into the air. Slowly rotate the bowl as you work. When all the sugar is blended in, spoon the mixture out onto the prepared baking sheet. Spread it out lightly without overworking it and leave the surface slightly rough; it levels out a little as it bakes.

For a less rustic appearance the meringue may be piped. Use a large plain nozzle and pipe contiguous concentric circles.

For small meringues work with 2 teaspoons and lay mounds about 1½ inches apart.

To give a sparkle, lightly dredge the meringue surface with sugar.

Dry the meringue out in the preheated oven. It will turn to a pale coffee color and feel very crisp. Check that the underside has also dried by tapping gently: it should have a hollow ring. If not, leave in the oven a little longer. Meringue takes anywhere from 1½ to 3 hours to dry out, depending on the size and thickness.

These light and crisp sheets of meringue keep well for several weeks when wrapped in foil. They are a perfect standby for an instant spectacular dessert.

GARNISHING SUGGESTIONS
One cup whipped cream covered with a layer of 3½ ounces of plain, dark chocolate, grated or flaked; or sandwich two sheets of meringue with a coffee-and-chocolate-flavored butter cream first (p. 18), and top with whipped cream flavored with 2 tablespoons coffee liqueur, and chocolate flakes.

Soft berries such as strawberries, raspberries, red currants, and loganberries taste delicious on a layer of kirsch-flavored whipped cream. You will need at least 1 pound of fruit for a 9½-inch meringue. (Leave a few fruits with their stalks for a decorative touch.) Mangoes cut in generous slices also blend well; scatter them with a few toasted flaked almonds.

In wintertime, the sharp tang of orange-flavored cranberries is a refreshing contrast to a whipped-cream base. Drop about 3 cups washed cranberries in a saucepan with 3 long strips of orange peel. Add about 1 cup water. Bring to a boil and gently simmer for a few minutes or until the berries start to pop. Remove from the heat and stir in ¾ cup superfine sugar and 2 tablespoons orange zest. Leave to cool, then chill. Remove the strips of peel before spooning onto the whipped cream.

HAZELNUT MERINGUE CAKE

Confound your guests with this mouthwatering confection composed of meringue, nuts, chocolate, and coffee. It is a handsome party piece that is relatively easy to prepare and cuts sparingly, for it is quite rich. Prepare the cake at least a day before it is needed.

Hazelnut meringue layers	*generous ¾ cup superfine sugar*
7 egg whites	*3 teaspoons potato flour or corn flour*
scant 1 cup superfine sugar	*½ cup unsalted butter, softened*
1 cup ground hazelnuts, toasted	**Almond praline**
Plain meringue layer	*2 tablespoons water*
2 egg whites	*½ cup granulated sugar*
scant ⅔ cup superfine sugar	*¾ cup almonds, blanched, toasted, and chopped*
Coffee cream filling	**To decorate**
3 tablespoons instant coffee powder or granules	*1 recipe thick chocolate icing (p. 19)*
¼ cup boiling water	*toasted almond halves*
8 egg yolks, lightly beaten	

275°F: 80–90 minutes.

Hazelnut meringue layers: Take four sheets of parchment paper and on each draw a circle 9½ inches in diameter. Place the papers on baking sheets.

Beat the egg whites until they hold firm, snowy peaks. Beat in half the sugar until the mixture is well blended and looks glossy. Sift over half the remaining sugar and one-third of the ground hazelnuts and gently fold them into the mixture, taking care not to lose any air. Fold in the rest of the sugar and half the remaining hazelnuts, followed by the rest of the nuts.

Spoon equal portions of the meringue mixture onto the circles marked on the parchment paper. (If you are unable to fit four meringue circles into the oven at a time, it is possible to prepare this cake in a rectangular shape 10 by 5 inches.) Lightly level out the mixture to the correct size. Bake in the preheated oven.

The meringues will still feel soft to the touch when removed from the oven, but will immediately become crisp. It is wiser to remove one at a time and to transfer them at once to a wire rack to cool. Strip off the papers when cold.

Plain meringue layer: Prepare a plain meringue layer. Follow the method above but omit the nuts. Spread on paper in the same way and bake in the preheated oven until dry and lightly colored, about 1 hour. Leave to cool on a wire rack.

Coffee cream filling: Spoon the coffee powder into boiling water, stir, and leave to infuse. Strain about three-quarters of the liquid into a double boiler or large heatproof bowl set over simmering water. (Reserve the rest to flavor the icing.) Stir in the egg yolks, sugar, and flour. Continue stirring over heat until the mixture thickens enough to hold a ribbon trail for a few seconds, then remove from the heat and allow to cool. Beat the butter until light and fluffy, then beat in the cooled coffee cream, spoon by spoon, until all is well combined.

Almond praline: Boil the water with the granulated sugar in a heavy saucepan until a caramel forms. Drop in the nuts and stir lightly to coat them with the caramel. When the mixture boils, pour it straight onto an oiled baking sheet, spread out, and allow to cool. Break the cold praline into pieces, then chop or grind to a coarse powder.

To assemble: Reserve about 3 tablespoons of the coffee-cream filling and divide the remainder into 4 portions. Sandwich together 5 layers of meringue with the filling. First, 2 layers of hazelnut meringue, then the plain layer, followed by the 2 other nut layers. Leave the top plain and coat only the sides of the cake with the reserved coffee cream. Press about three-quarters of the almond praline all around the sides.

Lightly cover the cake with plastic wrap and leave in the refrigerator overnight, so that the cake may settle and the flavors infuse.

Next day prepare the chocolate icing (p. 19) and flavor with the reserved coffee syrup.

Starting from the center, pour the icing gently around until the top is covered, tipping the cake stand a little from side to side so that some of the icing trickles over the edges onto the praline surface. Avoid using a knife to spread the icing, this spoils the finish. After a few moments stud the top with a few almond halves as decoration and throw a small amount of praline onto the iced sides of the cake. Hazelnut Meringue Cake keeps well for several days.

GERMAN APPLE CAKE

This is an unusually deep tart in which apple halves are sliced only halfway across their width so that they maintain their shape.

Pastry	½ cup sultanas
scant 1¼ cups flour, sifted	1 tablespoon rum
¼ pound butter, chilled and cubed	1½ pounds cooking apples
2 tablespoons superfine sugar	1 tablespoon lemon juice
1 egg, lightly beaten	¾ cup slivered almonds
2 tablespoons ice water	⅓ cup granulated sugar
Filling	5 tablespoons butter, softened
2 tablespoons butter, melted and cooled	1 teaspoon ground cinnamon

400°F: 35–40 minutes.

Prepare the pastry as described on p. 14. Wrap and chill it for 30 minutes. Brush an 8½-inch springform pan with some of the melted butter. Roll out the pastry and line the base of the pan and the full depth of the sides. Chill for 15 minutes.

Put the sultanas and rum in a small bowl and allow to soak while you prepare the apples. Peel the apples and cut in half, or quarters depending on their size. Remove the cores carefully. Cut ½-inch-deep incisions ¼ inch apart on the rounded side of each apple section, not quite through the thickness so that the shape is retained. Brush with a little lemon juice to prevent discoloration.

Brush the chilled pastry case with the rest of the butter. Fill each hollow left by the apple cores with sultanas and pack the apple pieces closely into the pan, cut side uppermost. Scatter the slivered almonds,

sugar, and cinnamon over the surface. Cut small pats of butter and distribute them evenly on top.

Bake in the preheated oven. After about 20 minutes, when the apples start to color, cover with foil and finish baking; they should hardly brown. Lift out of the oven and leave in the pan to cool on a wire rack. Offer whipped cream on the side.

VARIATION

You may prefer to replace the butter pieces that finish the apple cake with a custard cream topping. In this case, bake the apple cake, minus the butter pieces, for 20 minutes; pour over the prepared egg-custard topping and bake for 20–25 minutes more.

Egg Custard Topping

Beat together 2 egg yolks and ¼ cup superfine sugar until light and creamy. Whip 2 egg whites until they hold firm peaks and fold them into the yolk mixture, alternating with spoonfuls of sour cream and rum. You will need about ½ cup sour cream and 1 tablespoon rum. Use immediately, as instructed above. With this topping there is no need to cover the cake with foil.

APPLE STRUDEL

This famous Austro-Hungarian dessert has its origins in the Middle East. Strudel pastry is fine and paper-thin, composed of flour, water, a small amount of butter and an egg. It strongly resembles filo pastry, which is made only with flour and water—butter is spread between the filo sheets as the pie or cake is assembled; both pastries are then wrapped or rolled around a filling. Fillings may vary from savory vegetables or meat, to cheese, nuts, and fresh fruits. Probably the best known strudels contain apples or cherries.

Both strudel and filo pastries are quite difficult to make and need an experienced hand; however, both are available ready-made. This recipe uses filo dough. To make apple strudel, have the filling already prepared, the butter melted, and the baking sheets greased before unwrapping the dough. Filo dough dries out very

quickly once it is exposed to the air, so use half the number of pastry sheets at a time, leaving the rest tightly wrapped while you work. Filo keeps in the freezer for up to 2 months; after that it crumbles when it is defrosted and exposed to the air.

¾ cup sultanas	scant ⅔ cup granulated sugar
1 tablespoon dark rum	
⅔ cup coarsely ground hazelnuts or 1 cup dried bread crumbs	2 teaspoons ground cinnamon
	9 ounces unsalted butter, melted and cooled
¼ pound unsalted butter	
2 pounds cooking apples	**To finish**
4 teaspoons lemon juice	confectioners' sugar
1 pound or 12 sheets filo dough	

400°F: 30 minutes.

Drop the sultanas in the rum and leave to plump. Lightly fry the hazelnuts or bread crumbs in the butter until well coated; set aside to cool. Peel, core, and cut the apples into ¼-inch slices and sprinkle with lemon juice to prevent discoloration.

Lay a clean towel on the work surface and dust it with flour. Lay a sheet of filo dough on the towel and brush it all over with melted butter, quickly cover with a second sheet of filo and brush with butter as before. Continue layering and brushing the sheets of pastry with butter until everything is used, but reserve a little butter for finishing the strudel.

Scatter the toasted nuts or bread crumbs over about three-quarters of the pastry and carefully cover with the apple slices. Dredge a mixture of the sugar and cinnamon all over and finish with an even scattering of plumped sultanas. Using the tea towel as an aid, carefully roll up the strudel, tucking and folding in the sides so that the filling cannot escape. Transfer to the baking sheet, seam side down, and brush all over with melted butter. Bake until puffed and golden. Remove from the oven and dredge generously with confectioners' sugar.

Apple strudel tastes best served warm out of the oven, but it does keep well for a couple of days. Offer whipped cream on the side.

FRESH STRAWBERRY SPONGE CAKE

A simple but stunning dessert that should be prepared the day it is to be eaten.

Fat-free sponge	*2 tablespoons superfine*
5 eggs	*sugar*
scant ⅔ cup superfine	*1¼ cups whipped cream*
sugar	*5 tablespoons kirsch or*
2 inches vanilla pod, split	*orange liqueur*
¾ cup flour, sifted	*confectioners' sugar*
To finish	*apricot jam*
1½ pints fresh	
strawberries, washed and	
patted dry	

350°F: 30–35 minutes.

Line the bottom of a 9½-inch springform pan with paper, butter all over, and dredge with an equal mixture of superfine sugar and flour.

Prepare the fat-free sponge as described on p. 15, either by the classic method over heat or by the cold method. Bake and let cool. Reserve 5 whole strawberries with their stalks for decoration; hull and cut the remainder into slices. Fold the sugar into the whipped cream and flavor with 2 tablespoons of the kirsch or orange liqueur.

Finish the cake about 1 hour before serving. Strip off the paper and slice the cake into 3 equal layers.

Put the bottom sponge layer on a serving dish and sprinkle over about 1½ tablespoons kirsch or orange liqueur. Smooth over half the whipped cream and embed half the strawberry slices in it.

Cover with the second layer of sponge and press it down quite firmly. Sprinkle with the rest of the kirsch or orange liqueur, spread with the rest of the whipped cream, and cover with the remaining strawberry slices. Sandwich with the top sponge layer.

Arrange the reserved strawberries attractively on top of the sponge, using a dab of apricot jam to hold them in place. Keep in the refrigerator until needed. Dredge with confectioners' sugar over all just before serving.

TIRAMI-SÙ TORTE

Tirami-Sù Torte is a rich and delicious dessert. It is an interpretation, from the Italian part of Switzerland, of a Venetian favorite. The English translation, "pick-me-up," no doubt refers to the coffee and brandy it contains. The cake may be frozen for up to 2 months without the final dusting of chocolate. Defrost in the refrigerator overnight and decorate before serving.

Sponge
5 eggs
scant ⅔ cup superfine sugar
2 inches vanilla pod, split
¾ cup flour, sifted

Crème Pâtissière
1 cup milk, boiled
2 inches vanilla pod, split
¼ cup superfine sugar
3 egg yolks
1½ tablespoons flour, sifted
1½ tablespoons unsalted butter, melted and lightly browned
1 tablespoon dark rum

Tirami-Sù syrup
½ cup water
1 teaspoon instant coffee powder or granules
½ cup boiling water
scant ¾ cup granulated sugar
½ cup brandy

Tirami-Sù cream
1 teaspoon unflavored gelatin
1½ cups mascarpone or cottage cheese, drained and sieved
2 teaspoons orange zest
2 tablespoons orange juice, strained
½ cup whipped cream

To finish
cocoa powder

Sponge: Prepare the fat-free sponge as described on p. 15 with the eggs, superfine sugar, seeds from the vanilla pod, and flour. Line the bottom of a 9½-inch springform pan, butter it, and dust with equal amounts of superfine sugar and flour. Pour in the sponge mixture and bake until risen and golden. Allow to cool on a wire rack.

Crème pâtissière: Prepare as described on p. 70, using the quantities of ingredients given above. Rub a little butter over the surface to prevent a skin forming and set aside to cool.

Tirami-Sù syrup: Dissolve the coffee powder in the boiling water. Put ½ cup water and the sugar into a heavy-bottom pan, simmer first to dissolve the sugar, then bring to a boil and cook until the thread stage has been reached (see p. 18). Remove the pan from the heat, add the coffee mixture and the brandy; stir well to combine. Allow to cool.

Tirami-Sù cream: Dissolve the gelatin in 1½ tablespoons of almost-boiling water as described on p. 69. Place the mascarpone or cottage cheese in a bowl with the orange zest and orange juice. Blend in the cooled crème pâtissière.

Gently pour over the melted gelatin and stir in well. Finally fold in the whipped cream.

To assemble: Slice the sponge cake into 3 layers. Line the bottom of a 9½-inch springform pan with wax or parchment paper and lay into it the bottom layer of cake. Spread about one-third of the Tirami-Sù cream over and level the top. Place the second sponge layer on the cream filling and sprinkle thoroughly with half the coffee syrup. Cover with a second portion of cream and the remaining sponge layer. Soak the sponge with the rest of the syrup and spread the rest of the cream evenly all over. Cover the cake with plastic wrap and chill in the refrigerator for at least 4 hours, or until the cake has set.

To finish: Cut out a large cardboard star shape as a template for the middle of the cake.

Remove the spring sides of the pan from the cake and place the star in the center. Sprinkle cocoa powder all over the sides and on the surface of the cake quite thickly; carefully remove the cardboard template, leaving a white star in the middle. Slide the cake off the base onto a serving plate. Refrigerate until needed and serve cut into thin slices.

Roulade aux Marrons Glacés

A touch of luxury turns this simple sponge roll into an elegant temptation. It is possible to buy marrons glacés (glacé chestnuts) individually wrapped or in syrup. Use more than instructed if you wish to improve the flavor.

Sponge roll	3 tablespoons brandy or
½ cup superfine sugar	coffee liqueur
4 eggs, separated	4 marrons glacés,
1 teaspoon lemon zest	coarsely chopped
scant ¾ cup flour, sifted	**To decorate**
Filling	¼ cup chocolate coffee
2 cups heavy cream	beans (optional)

450°F: about 10 minutes.

Prepare a 14-by-10-inch jelly roll pan. Line the bottom of the pan with foil and leave a few inches overhanging the ends and sides. Butter generously and set aside.

Reserve 2 tablespoons of the sugar and place the remainder in a bowl with the egg yolks. Beat them together into a pale, creamy mixture, until the surface holds a ribbon trail for 5 seconds. Mix in the lemon zest.

In another bowl beat the egg whites until they hold firm, snowy peaks; beat in the reserved sugar until the mixture is slightly glossy. Lighten the egg and sugar mixture by mixing in 2 tablespoons of the beaten egg whites, then, alternating with spoonfuls of sifted flour, fold the rest in carefully.

Pour the mixture into the pan and smooth out lightly. Place in the preheated oven and bake until it is well risen, golden brown, and feels slightly springy to the touch.

Dredge a large sheet of wax paper with superfine sugar, turn the cake over onto it while still hot, and peel off the foil. Trim away the crisp, uneven edges. This makes it easier to roll. Cover with a second sheet of foil and roll the sponge from the short side into a loose roll. Lay on a wire rack, seam side down, and cover with a slightly damp cloth. Allow to cool.

Beat the cream into soft peaks and gently beat in the brandy or coffee liqueur. Continue to beat until it is firm. Reserve 2 tablespoons of the marrons glacés and fold the remainder into the cream.

Unroll the cold sponge and smooth three-quarters of the cream all over; roll up again. Smooth the rest of the cream all over the top and sides, scatter with the reserved marrons glacés, and decorate with chocolate coffee beans. Refrigerate before serving. This cake will stay fresh for 1–2 days.

Walnut, Coffee, and Rum Roulade

Walnuts have a special and distinctive flavor that is complemented by coffee. This nut-enriched sponge roll is quite soft in texture when baked; it must be well browned before any attempt is made to peel off the foil. The cake keeps well for 2–3 days in the refrigerator.

1 heaped teaspoon instant	**To finish**
coffee powder or granules	1¼ cups whipped cream
1 teaspoon boiling water	2 tablespoons dark rum
4 eggs, separated	or coffee liqueur
⅓ cup superfine sugar	1 tablespoon superfine
½ cup walnuts, coarsely	sugar
ground	confectioners' sugar

350°F: 15–20 minutes.

Line a 14-by-10-inch sponge roll pan with foil, letting the ends overhang by about 2 inches. Brush well with melted unsalted butter. Dissolve the coffee powder or granules in the water. Set aside to cool.

Beat the egg yolks and sugar in a bowl set over a pan of simmering water until it reaches the ribbon stage, when the mixture holds a trail for at least 5 seconds (see p. 15). Lift the bowl off the heat and continue beating while it cools and almost triples in volume. Beat in the cooled coffee liquid.

Beat the egg whites in a separate bowl until they stand in well-formed, snowy peaks; then, alternating with spoonfuls of ground walnuts, gently fold the beaten egg whites into the main mixture until all is well combined. Pour the mixture into the prepared pan and, using a spatula, level it out very lightly, making sure that all the corners are filled. Bake in the preheated oven until well browned, though still soft to the touch.

Immediately turn out onto a sugar-dredged piece of wax paper. Very carefully peel the foil off the back of the sponge, easing it with a knife if necessary. Trim the edges straight, cover with a clean sheet of parchment paper, and roll it up. Allow to cool on a wire rack covered with a slightly damp cloth.

The cake may be finished 3–4 hours ahead of time. It keeps well, and the flavors have more time to develop. Fold the sugar and rum or coffee liqueur into the whipped cream. Unroll the cooled walnut roll and spread a layer of cream all over. Roll up again and place, seam side down, on an elegant serving dish. Dredge the surface of the cake generously with confectioners' sugar just before serving.

SCHWARZWALDER KIRSCHTORTE

BLACK FOREST CHERRY CAKE

This is one of the most popular after-dinner desserts in Britain today. As yet there is no traditional recipe for it because it is still too young. Originating sometime in the last fifty years, and coming from southern Germany, where kirsch is distilled, it is made of chocolate sponge cakes, cherries, and whipped cream; and the cherry-flavored kirsch acts as a spirited cleanser for the rich ingredients.

Kirsch is not always readily available, but dark rum is an excellent alternative. In either case, be generous with it, for if too little is used, the flavor will be quite lost.

Chocolate sponge	2 tablespoons milk
1²⁄₃ cups flour	**Filling**
2 teaspoons instant coffee powder	1¹⁄₂-pound can or jar pitted morello or sour cherries
2 tablespoons cocoa powder	scant ¹⁄₂ cup cherry juice, strained
8 eggs, separated	³⁄₄ cup kirsch or dark rum
1¹⁄₃ cups superfine sugar	2 tablespoons superfine sugar
2 tablespoons vanilla sugar (p. 11)	2¹⁄₂ cups heavy cream, lightly whipped
3¹⁄₂ ounces plain dark chocolate, melted and cooled (p. 11)	**To decorate**
1 cup unsalted butter, melted and cooled	chocolate curls (see below)
3 teaspoons baking soda	

350°F: 45 minutes.

Chocolate sponge: Sift together the flour and coffee and cocoa powders; set aside. Beat the egg yolks and sugars until pale and fluffy and when some of the mixture dropped onto the surface leaves a trail for about 5 seconds (the ribbon stage, see p. 15). Mix in the cooled chocolate. Sift about one-third of the flour mixture across the top and, using a large metal spoon, fold it in carefully along with about one-third of the melted butter. Continue with the remaining flour and butter in two further batches. Beat the egg whites in a separate bowl until they form soft peaks. Fold gently into the mixture. Dissolve the baking soda in the milk and gently stir it into the finished cake mixture.

Have the bottoms of two 9½-inch springform pans ready lined with wax paper. Brush them with melted butter and dust with equal parts of superfine sugar and flour.

Divide the cake batter between the two pans and bake in the preheated oven. Leave to stand in the pan on a wire rack for a few minutes before turning out to cool. Strip off the papers.

Filling: Drain the cherries and set aside a few for decoration. Mix the cherry juice with ½ cup of the kirsch or rum, or more, to taste. Beat the sugar into the cream and fold in the remaining kirsch or rum.

To assemble: Slice each sponge into two layers. Sprinkle over one sponge a third of the kirsch syrup and cover with a quarter of the cream. Press half the fruit into the cream surface.

Cover with the second sponge, sprinkle with more syrup, spread a further quarter of whipped cream, and top with the rest of the cherries.

Lay the third sponge on top, sprinkle with the rest of the syrup, and cover with half the remaining cream. Top with the last sponge and smooth most of the remaining cream all over the top and sides.

Pipe a few rosettes of cream on top. Stud with the reserved cherries and decorate with the chocolate curls (see below).

Leave in the refrigerator to rest and for the flavors to mature for several hours, before serving.

Chocolate curls: Gently melt 3½ ounces plain dark chocolate in a small bowl set over simmering water; allow to cool for a minute. Pour it onto a lightly oiled surface (marble or Formica is best) and spread the chocolate out smoothly using a spatula, to about ⅛ inch thickness.

When it has set and only just cooled, take a large knife blade and hold it carefully at either end; sawing gently, pull the knife toward you—the slightly soft chocolate will curl or flake. Transfer to a sheet of wax paper to cool and harden.

These curls will store in an airtight container for several weeks.

GÂTEAU SAINT HONORÉ

Shortcrust pastry
¾ cup flour
pinch of salt
6 tablespoons butter, chilled and cubed
1 tablespoon superfine sugar
1 egg yolk
1 tablespoon ice water

Choux pastry
⅔ cup flour
pinch of salt
7 tablespoons butter, cubed
1 cup water
4 eggs, lightly beaten

Crème Saint Honoré
6 eggs, separated

2 tablespoons flour, sifted
pinch of salt
1 teaspoon lemon zest
1⅓ cups superfine sugar
1 cup milk, heated

Caramel
1 cup granulated sugar
3 tablespoons water

To finish
1 egg, lightly beaten
½ cup heavy cream, whipped
2 tablespoons superfine sugar
toasted slivered almonds

400°F: 10 minutes, then 375°F:
see recipe instructions.

Shortcrust pastry: Prepare the pastry, as described on p. 14. Chill for 30 minutes, then roll out into a ¼-inch-thick circle 9 inches in diameter. Lay on a buttered baking sheet and coat the outer edge with lightly beaten egg. Prick the pastry in the middle with a fork. Chill.

Choux pastry: Sift the flour and salt together, then again onto a sheet of wax paper. Drop the butter pieces into a pan with the water and set over gentle heat to melt and warm. When the butter has melted, increase the heat and bring the liquid to a rolling boil. Pour all the flour in at once and beat briskly over a reduced heat until the paste is smooth and rolls off the sides of the pan into a ball. Do not overcook. Draw aside and allow to cool for 5 minutes.

Beat the whisked eggs into the mixture a little at a time; there may be some left over since the texture should be elastic but quite firm. Beat the paste thoroughly until it has a glossy sheen.

To assemble: Spoon some of the mixture into a pastry bag fitted with a large, plain ½-inch nozzle and pipe a band of choux paste onto the egg-washed rim of the shortcrust pastry base. Brush with egg. Bake for 10 minutes, lower the temperature, and bake for about 20 minutes more, or until the choux pastry ring has browned well and puffed to about three times its original size. The pastry will also have colored. Remove from the oven, leave on the baking sheet, and set to cool on a wire rack. Prick the choux pastry ring in several places. Leave the oven on and raise the temperature again.

Place another baking sheet in the oven; this prevents the underside of the small choux buns from burning. Run cold water over a third baking sheet and shake off any excess. Pipe about 16 small walnut-sized buns onto the wet baking sheet about 1½ inches apart. Wash with egg. Place the sheet in the oven on top of the other baking sheet and bake for 20 minutes or so, until the buns are very well risen and golden brown. Lift out, prick each one with a fork to allow the steam to escape, and allow to cool on a wire rack.

Crème Saint Honoré: Beat the egg yolks well, then add the flour, salt, and lemon zest. Mix in half the sugar and the milk. Strain the liquid into a large bowl set over simmering water and heat the mixture to just below boiling (otherwise it curdles), stirring all the time. It should be like a thick custard. Pour into a bowl and set aside. Beat the egg whites into firm peaks, beat in half the remaining sugar, and then fold in the rest. Fold the meringue into the warm egg yolk mixture. Set aside to cool.

Whipped cream: Sweeten the whipped cream with the 2 tablespoons superfine sugar and fill each choux bun with a spoonful of cream.

Caramel: Heat the granulated sugar with the water and cook to a caramel. Plunge the pan base into water to cool it, then set the pan bottom in a bowl of hot water to keep the caramel liquid.

To finish: Spear each choux bun with a fork and dip the top in the caramel; stick the buns side by side on the choux pastry ring with a dab of caramel.

Spoon the cooled Saint Honoré cream into the cake hollow, scatter over a few toasted slivered almonds, and chill before serving.

DOBOSTORTE

This is undoubtedly the best-known Hungarian cake. Thin biscuit layers are sandwiched together with a rich chocolate-cream filling, and the top of the cake is coated with a sheet of caramel glaze. It takes quite some time to prepare but keeps well and cuts into many portions; and most important of all, it tastes delicious.

The cake should be assembled as soon as the layers have cooled, for they crisp and harden after a short time, which makes them more difficult to handle.

MAKES 14 SLICES

Biscuit layers

6 eggs, separated

scant 1 cup superfine sugar

¾ cup flour, sifted three times

Chocolate cream

1 cup unsalted butter, softened

4 ounces plain dark chocolate, melted and cooled (p. 11)

¾ cup superfine sugar

1 egg yolk

1 tablespoon dark rum

Caramel glaze

¾ cup granulated sugar

To finish

½ cup hazelnuts, coarsely chopped

425°F: 5–6 minutes.

Prepare 6 sheets of parchment paper and trace on each a 9½-inch circle. Place each on a baking sheet.

Biscuit layers: Beat the egg yolks and sugar together until pale and creamy, to the stage when some of the mixture dropped on the surface forms a ribbon trail for a few seconds. Beat the egg whites separately until they hold firm, snowy peaks, then fold them carefully into the yolk mixture, alternating with spoonfuls of sifted flour.

Carefully spread a thin, even layer of mixture on the circle marked on the parchment paper (you may bake two at a time) and bake until pale gold in color. Remove from the oven, and while the cake is still hot, invert a 9½-inch cake pan over it and trim an even edge all around. Transfer to a wire rack to cool. Bake 6 layers in all, in a similar fashion.

Chocolate cream: Beat the butter with the chocolate, sugar, and egg yolk; mix in the rum. Divide the chocolate cream into 6 portions.

To assemble: Set aside 1 biscuit layer, which is to be glazed with caramel later, and sandwich the other 5 layers with the cream, spreading a portion of cream over the top as well. Trim the sides even. Smooth the rest of the cream on the cake sides. Embed the chopped hazelnuts around the sides.

Caramel glaze: Generously butter a board a little larger than the cake and lay the remaining biscuit layer on it. Heat gently ⅓ cup of the granulated sugar in a heavy-bottom pan until golden, then add the remaining sugar and cook until it has thickened.

Pour immediately over the sixth biscuit layer and smooth all over quickly with a well-buttered knife. Cut through the caramel firmly, while still hot, without breaking the biscuit layer, and divide it into 14 equal slices. Trim away the rough edges of the caramel; allow to cool. Lift the caramel layer onto the top of the cake. Leave to mature for at least a day before cutting.

PUNSCHTORTE

This simple iced cake masks a colorful citrus- and rum-laced interior. Offer it to your guests with whipped cream on the side.

Sponge layers	¾ ounce plain dark
8 eggs, separated	chocolate, melted and
1 cup superfine sugar	cooled (p. 11)
scant 1½ cups flour, sifted	red and green food coloring
Punch syrup	**To finish**
¼ pound sugar cubes	2 tablespoons apricot
2 lemons, wiped clean	jam, warmed and
1 orange, wiped clean	strained
½ cup dark rum	punch icing (p. 19)
½ cup water	red food coloring
	glacé fruits and angelica

350°F: 30 minutes.

Sponge layers: Prepare the sponge batter as described on p. 15. Turn into two 9½-inch springform pans that have had their bottoms lined and greased, then coated with equal parts of flour and superfine sugar. Bake the sponges until risen and golden, then set them on a wire rack to cool.

Punch syrup: Rub the sugar cubes on the lemons and orange so that the oils of the zests are absorbed. Halve the fruits and squeeze and strain the juices. Mix together with the rum. Set aside. Drop the sugar cubes into the water in a heavy-bottom pan or a sugar boiler. Set over low heat and warm gently until all the sugar has dissolved. Turn up the heat and boil vigorously to the thread stage, 225°F (p. 18), which takes about 20 seconds of boiling.

Plunge the base of the pan into cold water for a moment, to arrest the cooking. Add the rum and citrus juices to the sugar syrup, replace on the heat, and boil up for a few moments so that the flavors blend. Reserve 1 tablespoon of punch syrup for the icing.

Spoon out 3 equal amounts of syrup into separate containers. To one add a drop of green food color. To the second add a drop of red color. Mix the melted chocolate into the third portion.

To assemble: Strip the papers off two sponges. Cut the center out of one sponge, leaving a 1-inch border. The removed inner portion is cut into dice about 1½ inches square. Divide the dice equally into 3 portions and soak each portion in one of the punch syrups.

Slice the remaining sponge into two layers and brush the base with the warm apricot jam. Set the sponge border onto the edge, making sure that the edge seals well. Pack the punch-soaked pieces of cake into the hollow close together, making an attractive pattern with the different colors. Cover the whole with the remaining sponge layer.

Line the base and sides of a cake pan with wax paper (so that the acid of the fruit syrup does not react with the metal) and lift in the reassembled cake. Cover and refrigerate overnight.

Prepare a punch icing (p. 19) and tint it pale pink with a drop of red food coloring. Spread the icing over the cake and decorate with glacé fruits and angelica.

CHILLED LEMON CHEESECAKE

This is a typical American-style cheesecake, on a bread crumb base. It is set with gelatin, and the light and fluffy texture makes it an ideal dessert to serve after a rich main course. Prepare it at least 2 days ahead of time.

Crumb base

scant 1 cup fresh-toasted bread crumbs or graham crackers, crushed

scant ½ cup superfine sugar

½ teaspoon ground cinnamon

½ teaspoon nutmeg

6 tablespoons butter

1½ tablespoons apricot jam

Filling

2 cups granulated sugar

½ cup water

6 egg yolks, well beaten

1½ tablespoons unflavored gelatin

6 tablespoons very hot water

1¼ cups lemon juice, strained

6 teaspoons lemon zest

1¾ cups cottage cheese, sieved

6 egg whites

To decorate

green grapes

thin lemon slices, cut and twisted

Crumb base: Line the bottom of a 9½-inch spring-form pan with parchment paper and oil the sides well. Mix the bread crumbs or crushed grahams with the sugar and spices. Melt the butter and apricot jam together and stir in the crumb mixture. Turn out into the baking pan and press firmly and evenly over the base, using the back of a spoon. Chill.

Filling: Gently heat the sugar in the water until dissolved. Raise the heat and boil the syrup to the soft ball stage (235°–245°F—a little syrup dropped into ice water forms a sticky, soft ball that loses its shape when removed from the water). Plunge the base of the pan into cold water for a moment to stop the cooking.

Immediately pour the syrup onto the egg yolks, beating all the time, and continue beating until the mixture cools. Transfer to a large bowl.

Dissolve the gelatin in the very hot water (just off the boil) and stir gently. If it does not dissolve properly, stand the container in a bowl of hot water. Strain the gelatin liquid into the egg mixture and mix in the lemon juice and zest. Allow to cool.

Fold the cottage cheese into the lemon cream carefully and set aside until on the point of setting. Meanwhile whisk the egg whites into creamy, firm peaks, then gently fold them into the mixture. Immediately pour this into the prepared pan and smooth the surface. Chill for at least 3–4 hours.

Carefully remove the pan and transfer the cheesecake to a serving dish. Decorate with thinly cut twists of lemon and halved and seeded green grapes.

69

SWEET PASTRY FRUIT FLAN

Sweet pastry flans, brimming with soft, fresh raspberries and strawberries or red currants, are among the most appealing of desserts. They taste even better with a layer of crème pâtissière or Crème Saint Honoré (p. 65) underneath. Berries are layered in baked pastry shells while other fruits, such as apricots, plums, and grapes, should be baked in the raw pastry case.

Pastry
scant 1¼ cups flour, sifted

pinch of salt

¼ pound butter, chilled and cubed

2 tablespoons superfine sugar

2 tablespoons ice water

1 egg, lightly beaten

To finish
1 egg white

Crème pâtissière
(optional)

2 inches vanilla pod, split

1 cup milk, boiled

¼ cup superfine sugar

3 egg yolks

1½ tablespoons flour, sifted

1½ tablespoons unsalted butter, melted and lightly browned

1 tablespoon rum or kirsch

Fruit filling
2 tablespoons ground almonds

2–2½ pints strawberries, raspberries, or red currants, lightly washed, hulled, and dried

Glaze
(optional)

3 tablespoons red currant jelly

2 tablespoons kirsch

400°F: 10 minutes, then 350°F: 20 minutes.

Pastry: Prepare the pastry, as described on p. 14. Wrap in plastic and chill for 30 minutes. Line with pastry the bottom and 1 inch up the sides of a lightly buttered 9½-inch flan tin. Prick all over with a fork.

Lay a sheet of wax paper or foil on top and weigh down with beans or pebbles.

Place the flan tin on a hot baking sheet in the preheated oven and bake as indicated, or until the pastry is golden. Remove from the oven and take off the paper and weights. Brush the surface with the lightly beaten egg white and dry out in the hot oven for 5 minutes. Allow to cool in the tin on a wire rack.

Crème pâtissière (optional): Drop the split vanilla pod in the hot milk and allow to infuse for 10 minutes. Beat the sugar with the egg yolks until pale and creamy and thick enough to hold a ribbon trail for a few seconds. Sift in the flour and stir to combine.

Remove the vanilla pod from the milk (wash and reserve for later use) and pour a small quantity over the egg mixture; blend well. Add this to the rest of the milk in the pan and replace over the heat. Continue beating hard on a brisk heat until the paste is thick and smooth and rolls off the sides of the pan.

Remove from the heat, fold in the browned butter and the rum or kirsch and pour into a bowl. Seal the top to prevent a skin from forming by pushing a small pat of butter across the surface.

To assemble: When the pastry shell is cold, scatter ground almonds over the base. Spoon in the cream, if used, and level the surface. Pack the prepared fruits in close together, arranging them carefully. Strawberries should have their points upward.

Glaze: A light glaze may be made by heating the red currant jelly and kirsch together and brushing lightly on the fruits. Chill before serving.

VARIATION

Black and green grapes and kiwi fruit also taste delicious layered on a pastry-cream base. Use 2 kiwi fruit and about 1½ pounds grapes. Wash and dry the grapes carefully; cut them in half and remove the pips. Peel the kiwi fruit and slice about ¼ inch thick. Pack the fruits alternately into the flan case close together in even circles. Glaze with 3 tablespoons of apricot jam (p. 11). Serve with whipped cream on the side.

Hazelnut Pastry with Fresh Raspberries

Fresh fruit desserts are always tempting, and raspberries combined with this crisp hazelnut pastry are no exception. The pastry may be made 2–3 weeks ahead of time, but must be stored in an airtight container, for it quickly softens once it is exposed to air. It is best not to use frozen raspberries, since they tend to be rather wet once defrosted and spoil the pastry.

¾ cup hazelnuts	2 tablespoons superfine sugar
7 tablespoons unsalted butter, cubed	2 tablespoons kirsch or light rum
1 cup flour, sifted	1¼ cups whipped cream
scant ½ cup superfine sugar	confectioners' sugar

To finish

1–1¼ pints fresh raspberries, lightly washed and dried

325°F: 10–15 minutes.

Toast the hazelnuts on a flat baking sheet in a 350°F oven for about 10 minutes. Shake the tray now and then to make sure that the nuts are browning evenly. When the brown skins start to darken and split, remove the tray from the oven. Leave the heat on and reduce the temperature as indicated above.

Remove the skins from the slightly cooled nuts by rubbing them gently in a clean cloth, then shaking the nuts in a coarse sieve. Replace in the oven and toast for a few minutes more until they are pale golden. Allow to cool. Reserve a few nuts and chop coarsely; grind the rest into a powder, taking care not to overgrind and release the bitter oils.

Sift the flour into a bowl, put in the butter, cut into small pieces, and, using the tips of the fingers, lightly rub together to a fine crumb texture. Fork in the sugar and the ground hazelnuts. Then gently press the mixture together by hand until it stays in a fairly compact ball. This may be a little difficult, for there is no liquid to help bind the mixture. Divide the dough in half. Roll each piece into a flat circle about 8 inches in diameter and ⅛ inch thick; transfer to a greased and floured baking sheet, patch any tears if necessary, and bake until faintly colored. The pastry will still feel slightly soft; avoid overcooking, because it scorches and develops a bitter taste. Remove from the oven and transfer to a wire rack, where the pastries will become crisp and harden as they cool.

Choose about 16 handsome fruits and reserve for decoration. Fold the superfine sugar and the kirsch or rum into the cream. Reserve 6 tablespoons for the top of the cake.

Assemble the cake 30 minutes before serving; do not refrigerate it. Lay one pastry base on a large serving plate; smooth the whipped cream all over it and embed with the fruits. Cover with the second pastry circle. Spoon the reserved cream into a pastry bag fitted with a ¼-inch fluted nozzle and pipe contiguous concentric circles in the center of the cake. Place the reserved raspberries around the outside close together. Scatter the chopped hazelnuts on the cream. Dredge a small amount of confectioners' sugar over the cake just before serving.

VARIATION

Red currants may be mixed with the raspberries to give a sharp and refreshing tang. Use equal quantities of each fruit in this case.

FLORENTINE ALMOND AND COFFEE CAKE

	Filling
3 tablespoons instant coffee powder or granules	1 recipe cooked butter cream (p. 18)
2 tablespoons boiling water	1 tablespoon coffee liqueur or brandy
4 eggs, separated	**To finish**
1/3 cup superfine sugar	3/4 cup whipped cream
1 teaspoon lemon zest	1 tablespoon superfine sugar
1/3 cup ground almonds	chocolate curls (p. 65)
2 tablespoons flour, sifted	mocha chocolate coffee beans

325°F: 1 hour.

Dissolve the coffee powder in the boiling water. Allow to cool. Beat the egg yolks and sugar together until light and fluffy. Mix in the lemon zest. Beat in half the coffee liquid and the almonds. Beat the egg whites in a separate bowl until they hold firm, snowy peaks; spoon about a quarter of the egg whites onto the cake batter and blend it in. This lightens the consistency. Tip in the rest of the whites and lightly fold them in along with the flour, taking care to retain as much air as possible.

Bake the mixture in a buttered and floured 8½-inch springform pan until risen and golden. Leave in the pan to settle for 10 minutes before turning out onto a wire rack to finish cooling.

Flavor the butter cream with the remaining coffee liquid and the coffee liqueur or brandy.

Slice the cooled cake into three layers. Smooth half the butter cream on the bottom layer, cover with the second piece of sponge, and spread with the rest of the butter cream. Lay the remaining layer of cake on top.

Fold the tablespoon of sugar into the whipped cream and smooth the cream all over the top and sides of the cake. Roughen slightly with a fork and decorate with chocolate curls and mocha chocolate coffee beans. Refrigerate until ready to serve.

FRESH APRICOT TART

Pastry	Filling
scant 1¼ cups flour, sifted	1½–2 pounds ripe apricots, halved and pitted
pinch of salt	1 tablespoon lemon juice
¼ pound butter, chilled and cubed	**To finish**
¼ cup superfine sugar	3 tablespoons confectioners' sugar, sifted
2 tablespoons ice water	3 tablespoons apricot jam, strained and warmed
1 egg, lightly beaten	

375°F: 50–60 minutes.

Prepare the pastry following the instructions given on p. 14. Chill. Roll out and line an 8½-inch flan tin and push the pastry 1 inch up the sides of the tin. Prick all over with a fork and chill while you prepare the fruit.

Rub the cut surfaces of the apricots with lemon juice to prevent discoloration. Lay the apricot halves slightly overlapping in circles in the chilled flan. Reverse each new circle to create an interesting pattern. Do not sugar the fruit at this point or the juices will be drawn out of the fruit and will soak the pastry. Bake on a hot baking sheet in the preheated oven.

Remove the flan from the oven and allow to cool in the tin set on a wire rack for 10 minutes; then slide the flan out of the tin onto the rack and dredge with the confectioners' sugar. Brush the whole fruited surface with the warm jam. It will cool into a glossy jelly. Serve cold with whipped cream on the side.

5

HOLIDAYS

Spiced breads, cookies, and cakes were traditional fare from the earliest days of baking. Spices, dried fruits, and nuts were the most coveted and costly ingredients, and baking was generally reserved for religious festivals. In Europe spiced honey cakes originated in the monasteries and convents, and in England gilded gingerbreads with religious significance were already found early in the twelfth century. Fruited cakes for wedding celebrations were known in the reign of Queen Elizabeth I, when small cakes made of currants, spices, eggs, milk, sugar, and flour were thrown at a bride.

The spices, nuts, dried fruits, and exotic perfumes brought along the Spice Road to Venice were carried overland across northern Europe. One of the principal trading towns on the route was Nuremberg. By the fourteenth century it had developed into a prosperous center with a lively team of local cake craftsmen.

The newly established "Lebkuchen" guild took full advantage of the highly desirable commodities and baked their special spiced cakes using honey gathered in the surrounding forests. Today Nuremberg lebkuchen are still famous and are exported throughout the world. The same type of cookies remain popular throughout the Teutonic lands and have now become

part of traditional Christmas baking in the family home as well.

Many festive cakes were made of yeast dough, too. Yeast baking was popular among the lower classes, who could not afford the luxurious ingredients in any great quantity. The dough was a perfect base into which spices and a few fruits and nuts might be kneaded. In Germany, stollen, which might vary from region to region, remained traditionally shaped and folded to represent Christ wrapped in swaddling clothes.

Switzerland, with its various Catholic and Protestant cantons, celebrates more feast days than almost any other country. The Swiss are especially fond of festivities, and appropriate cakes are always baked. Lying close to Italy, early pâtissiers were strongly influenced by the spiced Arab-style cuisine that developed there, and their predilection for sweetmeats is very evident.

Cakes with dried fruit are hardly known in France, although spiced gingerbread cakes were popular. In southern France the Epiphany gâteau des rois is one of the few festive cakes. It is a simple yeasted dough not unlike the Swedish saffron bread, decorated with a few glazed fruits, and it traditionally contains a silver coin. Northern Epiphany cakes are generally baked as a flat, tartlike galette filled with an almond paste, like

SIMNEL CAKE

Traditionally Simnel cake was baked for Mothering Sunday, and it is only relatively recently that it has come to be considered as an Easter cake. The twelve marzipan balls that usually decorate the surface are said to represent the twelve apostles. This cake has a layer of marzipan in the middle.

Fruit cake

5 ounces butter, softened

1 cup soft brown sugar

4 eggs, separated

½ cup ground almonds

1 tablespoon dark rum

1¼ cups flour, sifted

2 teaspoons mixed spice

1½ cups currants

¾ cup sultanas

½ cup candied orange and lemon peel, chopped small

Marzipan

2⅓ cups ground almonds

2 cups confectioners' sugar

1 large egg, well beaten

3–4 teaspoons orange-flower water, lemon juice, or rose water

To finish

2 tablespoons apricot jam, warmed with 2 tablespoons water, strained and cooled

1 egg yolk

confectioners' sugar

325°F: 2 hours, then 300°F: 30 minutes.

Prepare the marzipan, as described on p. 87, roll into a ball, wrap, and chill.

Line the base and sides of a deep, loose-bottomed 8-inch cake pan with parchment or wax paper; butter well.

Preheat the oven and a flat baking sheet while preparing the cake batter. Cream the butter and sugar together until pale and fluffy. Beat in the egg yolks one at a time, then add the almonds and the rum.

the gâteau Pithiviers. In the last century the bûche de Noël (Christmas log) has become a traditional French Christmas cake. It is a simple cream-filled sponge roulade with small Christmas decorations.

Festive baking in Britain has always tended to be of a heavily fruited nature, whether it be a familiar "plumb" cake, containing not a solitary plum but plenty of other dried fruits and citrus peels, for Christmas or for Easter, or a seventeenth-century mince pie, banned by the Puritans, who considered them to be idolatrous.

Throughout the centuries the cakes for holidays have barely changed, and although each country and each region may have its specialties, they are all very similar to each other. The magic spices and exotic influences of the Orient are as powerful today as they were centuries ago.

Sift together the flour and spice. Dredge 1 table-spoonful over the currants, sultanas, and candied peels and make sure all the fruit is well coated.

Lightly mix about one-third of the remaining flour into the egg mixture. Beat the egg whites in a clean bowl into firm peaks and lightly fold them into the main mixture, alternating with siftings of flour and portions of dried fruit and peels. Pour half the mixture into the prepared cake pan.

Sift confectioners' sugar onto a work surface and roll one-third of the marzipan into a 7-inch circle; lay it on top of the cake batter and gently press it down. Smooth over the remaining cake batter, leaving a small hollow in the middle.

Place the pan on the hot baking sheet and bake for 2 hours; now cover the cake with 2 sheets of wax paper to prevent the top from burning and reduce the temperature. When the cake starts to shrink away from the sides of the pan, test with a skewer to make sure that the center has cooked through. Leave the cake in the pan for 15 minutes before turning it out to cool on a wire rack.

To finish the cake, brush the surface with the apricot jam. Roll out the remaining marzipan and set it on top of the cake; trim neatly. Lightly indent with a wire mesh to form a pattern.

Roll the marzipan scraps into 12 small balls and attach them at regular intervals around the edge of the cake with a dab of beaten egg yolk. Brush over the whole surface with more egg yolk. Toast the marzipan layer under a hot broiler for 3–4 minutes to color it lightly, taking care not to allow it to burn. The cake will keep fresh for 2–3 months in an airtight container. Dredge lightly with confectioners' sugar before serving.

HOT CROSS BUNS

These aromatic and spicy buns appear only at Eastertime. While shop-bought hot cross buns are usually finished with a cross of short pastry, I prefer to cut a deep incision in the risen buns before baking.

MAKES 24

3½ cups bread flour, sifted	4 tablespoons butter, softened
1 ounce fresh yeast or 2 tablespoons dried yeast	⅓ cup soft light-brown sugar
scant 1 cup milk, warmed to 80°F	2 eggs, lightly beaten
1 teaspoon granulated sugar	¾ cup currants
1 teaspoon salt	**Glaze**
2 teaspoons mixed spice	2 tablespoons milk
	2 tablespoons superfine sugar

400°F: 15 minutes.

Prepare a sponge batter, as described on p. 16, with ¾ cup of the flour, the yeast, milk, and the granulated sugar. Cover and set aside to ferment, about 10 minutes.

Sift the remaining flour with the salt and spice into a large bowl, rub in the butter, and stir in the brown sugar. Add the yeast batter and the eggs, then mix and knead into a very soft dough. Add the currants and knead them in well, taking care to distribute them evenly through the dough.

Cover the bowl with a warm cloth or place in a lightly oiled plastic bag and leave to rise until doubled in bulk. This takes about 1 hour. Lightly butter 2 muffin pans and dredge with flour.

Punch back the risen dough and knead for a moment or two. Using a tablespoon, fill each muffin mold about two-thirds full and shape the dough into a round

77

ball. Smooth over the surface with the back of a knife. Incise 2 deep cross cuts into the top of each bun with the back of a large knife. Cover with plastic wrap and leave to rise again until doubled in volume. Bake immediately in the hot oven.

Five minutes before the buns are ready, boil the milk and sugar to a bubbling syrup, lift the browned buns out of the oven and leave to cool for about 5 minutes. Brush the surface of each bun with the syrup twice to give a shiny finish.

PUMPKIN PIE

Pumpkins ripen toward the end of October. Hollowed out and cut into grotesque faces, they make wonderful candlelit Halloween masks. The cooked and mashed pulp makes a tasty filling for the traditional American Thanksgiving Day dessert.

1 small pumpkin	*1 teaspoon ground ginger*
¾ cup light-brown sugar	*2 tablespoons brandy or*
¼ pound butter, softened	*sherry*
3 eggs, lightly beaten	*1 9½-inch sweet*
1 cup heavy cream	*shortcrust pastry flan*
½ teaspoon salt	*case, parbaked (p. 15)*

375°F: 25 minutes.

Peel and slice the pumpkin, discard the seeds, and boil in lightly salted water until soft; push through a food mill and mash to a puree. Measure out 2½ cups pumpkin puree.

Beat the sugar and butter together until light and fluffy; blend in the eggs; mix in the cream, pumpkin puree, salt, ginger, and brandy or sherry. Pour the mixture into the parbaked pastry case and bake until it has puffed slightly. The center will appear to be not quite set. Serve warm or at room temperature, because it loses the flavor when chilled.

GINGERBREAD

Ginger, along with various other spices, came originally from India and China. Spices were carried west by explorers and the Crusaders. Later vast trading empires developed as the demand for spices increased dramatically.

Spiced breads were the traditional fare for all religious and secular celebrations, and gingerbread is said to be one of the oldest cakes in the world. In Europe it originated in the monasteries and convents, and a

78

little later in England it was also baked in the kitchens of the royal court. Early versions of gingerbread, made with honey, were quite hard and biscuity in character and were usually molded and cut into small sculptured shapes. Sponge ginger cakes only appeared in the seventeenth century with the introduction of molasses.

The following recipe is based on an old American gingerbread cake. It is usually baked in a deep square or rectangular pan.

MAKES 16 PIECES

6 tablespoons butter, softened	1 heaped tablespoon ground ginger
½ cup muscovado or dark brown sugar	1½ teaspoons ground cinnamon
½ cup molasses	1½ teaspoons ground nutmeg
scant ½ cup golden syrup	2 eggs, well beaten
scant ½ cup milk, warmed	juice and zest of 1 large orange
3 tablespoons sherry	1 teaspoon baking soda
1¾ cups flour, sifted	1 tablespoon warm water
1 teaspoon cream of tartar	

350°F: 35–40 minutes.

Beat the butter and sugar together until thick and fluffy. Mix in the molasses, syrup, milk, and sherry. Sift the flour together with the cream of tartar, ginger, cinnamon, and nutmeg. Mix alternating spoonfuls of the flour mixture and the eggs into the creamed ingredients. Add the orange juice and zest. Finally, dissolve the baking soda in the warm water and blend into the mixture.

Pour the batter into a buttered 12-by-8-by-1½-inch cake pan and bake until well risen. Leave in the pan to cool on a wire rack. Cut into squares before serving.

SPICY SPECULAAS

Speculaas is a traditional pre-Christmas sweetmeat offered in Holland at the feast of Saint Nicholas on December 6. Sinterklaas, sitting astride his white horse, dressed in red, fills the boots and shoes of the good children with gifts (the naughty children, it is said, are carried back to Spain in his sack). Meanwhile his gaily clad black attendant, Zwarte Piet, offers peppermint-drop cookies and molded shapes of Saint Nicholas as well as speculaas, dolls, and gingerbreads.

MAKES 40 PIECES

Pastry	scant ⅔ cup superfine sugar
1¾ cups flour	1 teaspoon lemon zest
1 teaspoon ground cinnamon	2 small eggs, beaten
½ teaspoon ground nutmeg	**Almond paste**
pinch of ground cloves	1½ cups confectioners' sugar
pinch of ground ginger	2⅓ cups ground blanched almonds
pinch of ground cardamom	1 large egg, well beaten
pinch of black pepper	3–4 teaspoons lemon juice
¼ teaspoon baking powder	**To finish**
pinch of salt	1 egg, beaten
5 ounces butter, softened and cubed	½ cup blanched almond halves

350°F: 35 minutes.

Sift the flour with the spices, baking powder, and salt two or three times. Drop in the butter pieces and rub to a fine crumb texture. Stir in the sugar and lemon zest, then add the beaten eggs and blend to a smooth pastry. Gather into a ball, wrap in plastic, and leave to rest in a cool place for several hours.

Make the almond paste, as described on p. 87, wrap, and chill until needed.

Roll out the pastry to about ⅛-inch thickness and cut 2 pieces to fit a 12-by-8½-by-1½-inch baking tray. Put one pastry layer in the bottom of the buttered tray.

Sprinkle a work surface with confectioners' sugar and roll out the almond paste to the same size as the pastry. Lift it into the pastry in the tray and cover with the second layer of pastry.

Brush with the beaten egg, score the surface with a trellis pattern, and stud each diamond shape with an almond half. Brush the surface again with egg. Bake until golden. Cool in the pan on a wire rack.

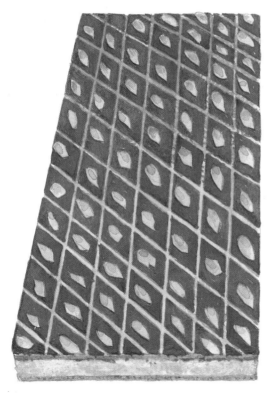

SWEDISH SAFFRON BREAD

Saint Lucia, the Swedish festival of light, is the children's celebration that falls on December 13. The youngest girl in the household rises before 6:00 a.m., dresses herself in white, and dons a crown of lingonberry greens studded with candles. She then visits her parents and the animals in the home bearing gifts of saffron yeast buns and coffee.

The dough may be plaited into a loaf or shaped into buns. The bread keeps fresh for 2–3 days.

MAKES 2 LOAVES

½ teaspoon saffron threads	1 egg yolk
1½ cups milk, warmed to 80°F	⅓ cup blanched almonds, chopped
6 tablespoons butter, melted	½ cup raisins
2⅔ cups bread flour, sifted	4 tablespoons candied orange and lemon peel, chopped
pinch of salt	**To decorate**
½ cup superfine sugar	1 egg, lightly beaten
½ ounce dry yeast or 1 ounce fresh yeast	granulated sugar
	chopped almonds or raisins

400°F: 20–25 minutes.

Prepare a sponge batter, as described on p. 16. Mix together 1 cup of the warmed milk, ¾ cup of the flour, 1 teaspoon of the sugar, and the yeast. Set aside for about 10 minutes to ferment and double in bulk.

Dry the saffron threads in the oven set at 275°F for a few minutes, then crush them into a fine powder. Stir the powder into the remaining milk and mix in the melted butter. Sift the flour and salt into a bowl, stir in the saffron mixture, the remaining sugar and the egg yolk, and finally the yeast mixture and combine well.

Continue working the dough and kneading hard until it is very smooth, elastic, and rolls off the sides of the bowl. (For more detailed notes on handling yeast dough, see pp. 16–17.)

Add the almonds, raisins, and candied peels and knead well until the fruits are evenly distributed. Place the dough in a large, lightly oiled plastic bag or in a mixing bowl covered with a cloth and leave to rise in a warm, draft-free place.

When the dough has doubled in bulk, punch it back on a floured surface and knead again until it is smooth. Cut in half and leave one piece covered while you finish the other.

Cut the dough into 2 equal pieces and roll each into a rope about 18 inches in length. Twist the two pieces together very lightly and loosely and tuck both ends under. Finish the second piece of dough in the same way. Transfer the loaves to buttered baking sheets, cover with a dry tea towel, and leave to rise until doubled in bulk again, about 40 minutes.

Brush each plaited loaf with the beaten egg and scatter the coarse sugar and a few chopped almonds or raisins over the surface. Bake immediately until well risen and golden brown. Serve cut into slices spread with unsalted butter.

This recipe can also be made easily with quick-rising yeast. If substituting, please follow the instructions on the yeast package.

SPICY LEBKUCHEN FOR CHRISTMAS

Lebkuchen are spicy nut cookies prepared at Christmastime in Austria, Germany, and Switzerland. Probably the best known are from Nuremberg; the town had already gained a reputation for the finest lebkuchen by the fourteen century. The local tradesmen established a lebkuchen manufacturers' guild and developed an extensive and lucrative trade in the luxury sweetmeats.

Lebkuchen are dried overnight before they are baked.

MAKES 60 PIECES

3 egg whites	1 teaspoon ground cinnamon
1½ cups confectioners' sugar, sifted	½ teaspoon ground cloves
1¼ cups unpeeled almonds, ground a little coarsely	60 thin wafer cookies
2 ounces plain dark chocolate, grated	**Chocolate icing**
	2 ounces plain dark chocolate
4 tablespoons candied orange and lemon peel, chopped small	½ cup confectioners' sugar
	1 tablespoon hot water

350°F: 25 minutes.

Beat the egg whites in a large bowl until they stand in firm, snowy peaks. Dredge over one-third of the confectioners' sugar and continue beating, adding the remaining sugar in two further stages, blending it in well until the meringue is thick and glossy.

In another bowl mix together the almonds, chocolate, peels, and spices, taking care that the fruits are separated and well coated with nuts and chocolate. Tip the mixture onto the meringue and, using a large metal spoon, fold the two together.

Cut the wafers into hearts, squares, or star shapes with a sharp-pointed knife. Mound some of the nut meringue onto the middle of each wafer, about ¾ inch high, and taper it down smoothly to the sides. Lay them quite close together on a baking sheet. Leave in the kitchen to dry and set overnight.

Next day preheat the oven before baking the lebkuchen.

Make the icing by melting the chocolate with 1½ tablespoons water. Gently stir to combine. Sift the confectioners' sugar into a clean bowl and slowly stir in the hot water, then stir in the melted chocolate to make a smooth mixture that coats the back of the spoon. Cover the bowl with a damp cloth to prevent the icing from drying out.

Bake the lebkuchen until the edges have colored slightly and lay them on a wire rack.

When they are cool enough to handle, dip the top of each into the chocolate icing to coat it; the heat of the lebkuchen will set the icing as it cools. With a skewer, pierce a hole through each one before it has cooled.

The lebkuchen will keep for several weeks stored in an airtight container, or thread colorful strings through the holes and hang them on the Christmas tree as decorations.

ALMOND STOLLEN

Stollen are a Christmas specialty from central Germany. This traditional bread was prepared and kneaded by hand at home in large quantities, and the unbaked loaves were then carried to the baker's around lunchtime. Early the same evening the housewives, accompanied by their offspring, would reassemble and patiently wait their turn as the baker carefully lifted tray after tray of aromatic loaves from his ovens.

Needless to say, a competitive element crept in as each loaf was identified; those that had risen perfectly were greeted with cheers and congratulations, while others that had collapsed dismally, much to the shame and disappointment of their owners, were subjected to good-tempered teasing.

MAKES 2 LOAVES

2 cups raisins	¾ pound butter, softened
⅔ cup mixed candied orange and lemon peel, chopped small	1 egg, beaten
	1 egg yolk
1 cup sultanas	2 teaspoons lemon zest
3 tablespoons dark rum	**Marzipan**
scant 1 cup milk, heated to 80°F	1⅓ cups confectioners' sugar
2 ounces dried yeast or 3½ ounces fresh yeast	1⅔ cups ground almonds
	1 egg yolk
1 cup superfine sugar	2 teaspoons lemon juice
7 cups bread flour, sifted	**Topping**
1 teaspoon salt	7 tablespoons unsalted butter, melted
¼ teaspoon ground ginger	½ cup granulated sugar
½ teaspoon ground cardamom	2 tablespoons vanilla sugar (p. 11)
½ teaspoon ground nutmeg	1 cup confectioners' sugar, sifted

400°F: 45–60 minutes.

Assemble the raisins, mixed peels, and sultanas in a bowl, stir in the rum and leave to swell overnight in a warm place.

Make a sponge batter, as described on p. 16, with the milk, yeast, 1 teaspoon of the sugar, and ½ cup of the flour. Cover and set aside to rise. Sift the remaining flour, spices, and salt into a large bowl, cut in the butter and rub together to a rough texture.

Make a well in the center, add the yeast batter, and blend with the flour, then mix in the beaten egg and the egg yolk, the remaining sugar, and the lemon zest.

Drain any liquid from the soaked fruits and add that too. Beat together well and start kneading, either in the bowl or on the floured work surface, until the dough is very firm, smooth, and elastic, throws large air bubbles, and starts to roll off the sides of the bowl. Cover the bowl with a warm tea towel and leave to rise in a warm place until it has doubled in bulk. This may take several hours.

Prepare the marzipan filling with the confectioners' sugar, almonds, egg yolk, and lemon juice, as described on p. 87, roll into 2 balls, wrap, and chill.

Punch back the risen dough, knead again for a few moments, pull the sides over into the center, turn it over, and replace in the bowl. Cover and leave to rise again for at least 30 minutes more, or until it doubles in bulk again.

Dust the work surface with flour and turn the risen dough out onto it. Flatten slightly and scatter the plumped fruits all over. Knead them in carefully, making sure that they are well distributed. Divide the dough into two equal pieces, leaving one covered while you finish the other.

Roll out the dough into a slightly flattened, oval shape large enough to fit onto the length of a baking sheet and almost half its width again, but leaving enough space to allow it to grow. With a rolling pin, press lightly across the full width, from the center outward on one side only.

Roll out one of the marzipan pieces about two-thirds the size of the flattened side and place it on top of the dough. Brush the remainder of the dough with a little water and fold the marzipan-covered side over twice into a crease and onto the uncovered part, leaving a margin of about 2 inches as a border—this also allows the dough to rise. Press together well to bind it. This rolling and folding technique is traditional for stollen and is said to represent the Infant Christ wrapped in swaddling clothes.

Cover the stollen and leave to rise again in a warm place, until doubled in bulk, about 30 minutes. Finish the second loaf in a similar way.

Carefully brush the entire surface of the stollen with about half the melted butter before baking. Remove from the oven when well risen and browned, which takes from 45 to 60 minutes depending on the size. Brush while still warm with the rest of the butter and sprinkle a mixture of the granulated, vanilla, and confectioners' sugar over the top to form a thick, sugary crust. When cold, wrap tightly in foil. Keep for 2–3 days before cutting. Stollen keeps fresh for several weeks.

MINCEMEAT

Early mincemeat pies usually contained meat, marrow, or suet as well as dried fruits, nuts, and spices. Today, suet is the only reminder of the past. Brandy is a vital ingredient, and the more that is used the longer the mincemeat will keep. Store for at least 1 month before using.

MAKES 5 POUNDS

¾ pound Cortlandt apples, peeled, cored, and chopped small	1 cup blanched almonds, chopped
½ pound shredded beef suet	1⅓ cups muscovado or dark brown sugar
1½ cups seedless raisins	1 teaspoon mixed spice
1½ cups currants	1 teaspoon ground nutmeg
2 cups candied orange and lemon peel, chopped	zest and juice of 1 lemon
	1¼ cups brandy

Combine the apples, suet, dried fruits, and almonds in a bowl. Add the sugar, spices, lemon zest, and juice and finally the brandy. Mix very thoroughly. Pack the mincemeat tightly into a bowl and seal closely. Set in a cool place and stir each day for a week, adding a little more brandy if all the liquid has been absorbed. Spoon the mixture into sterilized glass jars, seal as for jam, and store in a dark, cool place.

MINCEMEAT TARTS

MAKES 12

Sweet shortcrust pastry

scant 1¼ cups flour, sifted

pinch of salt

2 tablespoons superfine sugar

1 teaspoon lemon zest

2 tablespoons ice water

1 egg, lightly beaten

¼ pound butter, chilled and cubed

mincemeat

To finish

1 egg yolk, lightly beaten

superfine sugar

425°F: 15 minutes.

Make the pastry as described on p. 14. Roll into a ball and chill. Lightly butter 12 individual tart pans. Roll out the pastry to ⅛-inch thickness and cut 12 circles a little larger than the molds. Press each into a tart pan.

Spoon a generous amount of mincemeat into each pastry case, taking care not to overfill, and brush the pastry edges with water. Cut 12 more pastry circles from the remaining scraps to fit on top as lids and press them into place, making sure that the sides have sealed.

Make a small cross in the center of each tart with a knife, brush over with the lightly beaten egg yolk and dredge with the superfine sugar. Leave to settle for 30 minutes before baking.

When baked to an attractive golden color, turn out to cool on a rack.

BRANDY BUTTER

Brandy butter is delicious served with mincemeat tarts.

½ cup unsalted butter, softened

1 cup confectioners' sugar, sifted

3 tablespoons brandy

½ teaspoon lemon juice

pinch of ground nutmeg

Cream the butter and sugar together until pale and fluffy; mix in the brandy and lemon juice and blend very thoroughly. Add the nutmeg according to taste. Cover and leave to mature for 2 or 3 days.

TRADITIONAL ENGLISH CHRISTMAS CAKE

1 cup mixed candied peel, chopped

½ cup glacé cherries, washed and quartered

1 cup almonds, blanched and chopped

3 cups currants

3 cups sultanas

2¼ cups raisins

¾ cup brandy

10 ounces unsalted butter, softened

2 cups light or dark brown sugar

zest of 1 orange

zest of 1 lemon

6 eggs

2½ cups flour, sifted

½ teaspoon salt

½ teaspoon ground cloves

½ teaspoon ground nutmeg

1 teaspoon ground cinnamon

pinch of ground ginger

Marzipan

2 cups confectioners' sugar

2⅓ cups ground blanched almonds

1 large egg, well beaten

3–4 teaspoons lemon juice

To finish

5 tablespoons apricot jam, warmed and strained

1 cup mixed candied fruits

2 cups walnuts, pecan halves, or Brazil nuts

325°F: 20 minutes, then 300°F: 40 minutes, then 275°F: approx. 3¼ hours.

Assemble the mixed peel, cherries, almonds, currants, sultanas, and raisins in a large bowl. Add the brandy and stir well. Leave to macerate overnight.

Beat the butter and sugar together until pale and fluffy, mix in the grated citrus zests. Beat in 1 egg at a time thoroughly. If the mixture should start to curdle, sift over 1 or 2 tablespoonfuls of the flour. Sift the remaining flour with the salt and spices, 2 or 3 times. Strain the soaked fruits and reserve the liquid.

Combine the flour, spice, and alcohol with the main mixture, then stir in the brandied fruits. This mixture may rest overnight in the refrigerator.

Prepare a 9-inch loose-bottomed deep cake pan. Line the base and sides with 2 layers of wax or parchment paper, and finish with a third sheet that stands to form a 2-inch-high collar above the side of the pan. Grease well with butter.

Pour the mixture into the pan; smooth the surface and hollow out the middle slightly so that the cake bakes flat. Place the pan on a baking sheet that has been lined with 2 sheets of brown paper to protect the base. Bake as instructed.

If the top appears to be browning too quickly, cover with a sheet of wax paper. Test the cake for readiness; a skewer should come out dry. Lift out of the oven, set on a wire rack in the pan and leave to cool. Next day, turn out of the pan, strip off the papers, wrap in foil and store in an airtight pan. Let the cake mature for at least 3–4 days before finishing.

Christmas cake may be made well ahead of time and improves greatly if "fed" with brandy each week before the holiday. Prick the base with a fork and spoon over 2 tablespoons of brandy.

Do not cover with marzipan until about a week before Christmas.

Marzipan: Sift the confectioners' sugar into a bowl and add the almonds. Mix in the egg and lemon juice and beat well. Turn out onto a board sprinkled with confectioners' sugar. Knead to a smooth paste. Wrap and chill. Reserve one-third of the marzipan and roll the remainder on a sheet of wax paper dusted with confectioners' sugar. Cut into a circle about ½ inch larger than the cake. Roll out the rest of the marzipan into a long strip to cover the sides.

To finish: Slice away a thin layer of cake to level the top if necessary. Coat the cake all over with 3 tablespoons of the warm apricot jam. Invert the cake onto the marzipan circle and press in gently; fold over the edges and smooth down. Roll the sides of the cake over the long strip of marzipan. Smooth over with a rolling pin. Leave to dry out for several days before finishing. Decorate the cake with candied fruits and nuts and finish with the remaining apricot glaze.

SCOTTISH BLACK BUN

A traditional Scottish Twelfth Night black bun has a heavily fruited filling that is usually wrapped in a paste of butter-enriched bread dough. Like most festive pastries, it is baked in large quantities, and this recipe is made in two 1-pound loaf pans.

MAKES 2 LOAVES

Yeast dough

about 1¼ cups water, warmed to 80°F

2 tablespoons dried yeast or 1 ounce fresh yeast

3½ cups bread flour, sifted

1 teaspoon salt

5 ounces butter, softened and cubed

scant 1¼ cups strong white flour, sifted

Filling

6 cups currants

4½ cups sultanas

¼ cup preserved ginger, finely chopped

¼ cup whiskey

3 tablespoons butter, softened

¼ cup soft brown sugar

1½ tablespoons ground mixed spice

1 teaspoon ground ginger

1 teaspoon ground cinnamon

2 tablespoons molasses

1 inch vanilla pod, scraped

1¼ cups unpeeled almonds, coarsely chopped

To finish

1 egg, beaten

1 tablespoon whiskey

350°F: 2½–3 hours.

Prepare a sponge batter, as described on p. 16, with the water, yeast, ¾ cup of the flour and 1 teaspoon sugar taken from the main recipe. Cover and leave to ferment. Sift the remaining flour and salt into a large bowl, add the risen batter, and beat together well, then knead until the dough is smooth, elastic, throws large bubbles of air, and rolls off the sides of the bowl.

Cover with a warm cloth or place in a large, lightly oiled plastic bag and leave to rise and ferment to about double in size.

Meanwhile, assemble the currants, sultanas, and ginger pieces with the whiskey in a bowl and leave to soak. Cream the butter, sugar, and spices together until fluffy. Mix in the molasses, vanilla seeds, and chopped almonds. Set aside.

Punch back the risen bread dough, blend in the cubes of butter, and enough flour to make a workable, elastic dough. Cut off a piece of dough about ¼ pound in weight and cover the rest while you quickly finish the filling.

Add the whiskey-soaked fruits and the small piece of dough to the spiced sugar and butter mixture and mix thoroughly, kneading if necessary.

Roll out two-thirds of the reserved dough and line the bottom and sides of 2 buttered 1-pound loaf pans. Trim the edges. Fill each pan with half the fruited mixture and smooth the top. Roll out the rest of the dough and cut 2 rectangles to cover the filling. Moisten the edges of the dough in the pans with cold water and press and pinch firmly to make a tight seal. Pierce the cakes all the way through to the base in 4 places with a skewer, and prick only the surface with a fork. Brush with the beaten egg. Leave the cakes to rise and prove for about 30 minutes, then bake in the preheated oven.

When well browned remove from the oven, set on a wire rack, and immediately brush the tops of the black buns with the remaining beaten egg and whiskey mixed together.

When cold, wrap in plastic and store in an airtight container. Serve in thin slices.

INDEX

641.8653 M214c
Maher, Barbara.
Classic cakes and cookies

WITHDRAWN

Arlington County Public Library
Arlington, Virginia

17 756 561

CENTRAL LIBRARY
Arlington County, VA
Public Library
DATE DUE

CENTRAL LIBRARY
Arlington County, VA
Public Library
DATE DUE

NOV 2 6 1994
JUN 2 0 1995
AUG 2 7 1995
DEC 0 4 1995
OCT 0 6 1996
NOV 1 2 1997
JUN 2 4 1998
JUL 0 9 1998
NOV 2 8 1998
FEB 2 3 1999
R MAR 1 6 1999